Fictional
Religion

Fictional *Religion*

Keeping the New Testament New

Jamie Spencer

POLEBRIDGE PRESS
Salem, Oregon

Cover: Rembrandt's painting of the Prodigal Son.
Cover and interior design by Robaire Ream

Library of Congress Cataloging-in-Publication Data
Spencer, Jamie, 1945-
  Fictional religion : keeping the New Testament new / Jamie Spencer.
    p. cm.
  Includes bibliographical references and index.
  ISBN 978-1-59815-032-2 (alk. paper)
  1. Bible and literature. 2. Christianity and literature. I. Title.
  PN56.B5S69 2011
  820.9'3823–dc23
                                                        2011026319

To my Wife, Anna, whose life of thoughtful prayer
is a daily source of inspiration for me.

And to Kate, my loving daughter and a long-serving,
dedicated Acolyte.

Table of Contents

Introduction

Three interconnected claims will guide this book. Together, they should, I hope, be cause for celebration.

The first is one with which, I am confident, most sensible thinkers and believers would concur. It is this: the books of the New Testament are not the infallible Word of God. No, they are rather the inspired words of devout and humble writers, caught up in the fervor of a radically new understanding of the faith they inherited. The second claim is a corollary: those texts were in a state of flux during the faith's early centuries. Different sets of writers or officials were compiling competing anthologies of what they claimed, and in some cases insisted, was holy writ. Meanwhile, often unreliable scribes were at work, erasing or modifying theology they considered suspect; they would also make way for additions that took the form of narratives. Stories.

The third, perhaps more extravagant, proposition follows from these. I contend that we can and should build on that flexible tradition, turning to other, later stories, penned over many centuries by creative artists. In them, I submit, we can discover, and profit from, comparably inspired Christian doctrine, doctrine suitably adjusted to the new worlds which were shaping those artists. Throughout the Christian era, a vibrant legion of playwrights, poets, and story writers have performed the same services for New Testament doctrine that the Old Testament prophets and story-tellers provided for Jewish Law laid down in the Pentateuch. *Our* creative artists were never allowed entry into approved holy writ, but they have been shaping Christian doctrine and insights in new ways to meet new human conditions ever since the faith's founding. They have kept that new testament new.

Those four early gospels (and others, like that of Thomas, that fell by the wayside) each sought to embody and proclaim the young church's evolving evangelical needs. As a group, they reflect a diverse array of faith communities. Arthur Dewey, Professor of Religion at Xavier University and scholar of the Westar Institute, has noted that the gospel writers did not think alike. They "featured a plurality of ways to remember Jesus" (2009). That early pattern has continued ever since. Every era evolves new conventions, particular social habits and customs, distinctive cultural assumptions; each such era produces answerably distinctive creative literary artists. It is to them we can look for doctrinal modification and reinterpretation.

The writers considered in this volume were rarely certified theologians or ecclesiastics, (though a few were). Nevertheless, they wrestled with the faith they had inherited just as intensely and wrote about it just as persuasively, and expressed those insights in strikingly innovative fashion.

Sacred or Profane? Does it Matter?

The story of the woman taken in adultery, most scholars agree, was an insertion into John's gospel four centuries after the execution of that fictional tale's hero (8:1–11). That fact confirms the gospels' flexibility; Holy Writ opened its pages to at least one eloquent tale. The story's irresistible literary power and doctrinal acuity demanded inclusion, an intellectual process we can and should extrapolate even more widely. To test my proposition that secular literature can inspire as deeply as approved Writ, let us pair a verifiably original parable of Jesus himself with the work of a much later, genuinely secular, and indeed highly commercial writer. Let us see whether Luke's late first-century account of the Prodigal Son and Charles Dickens' dramatic portrait of Ebenezer Scrooge's revelatory Christmas morning, a mid-nineteenth-century invention, convey comparable doctrinal insights.

In the account of the Prodigal Son, the gospel writer dramatizes the new order promised in God's imperial realm; he announces how different things will be there when "thy kingdom come[s]." The older son in the tale rightfully resents the feast his father is throwing for his wayward but remorseful sibling. Without the brother's presence, incidentally, the tale becomes merely a festive celebration of a wayward sinner's return, a reassuring allegory about God's always-available forgiveness; with his presence, Luke's more complex message comes alive: conventional ethical expectations and practices, even including as fundamental a "right" as primogeniture, are now to be superseded. The parable is a reminder of just how revolutionary were Jesus' teachings, both for the family and for the wider culture. Luke sees that forgiveness cancels conventional, worldly complaints like those of the "good" son. Redemption and forgiveness are actions of the spirit and proclaim God's new kingdom; they trump merely human custom and social convention.

Now Scrooge. Like the wayward son of the parable, that flinty, old miser has gone through a dark night of self-loathing. His incisive, repentant words to his Third Visitor, "Spirit, hear me; I am not the man I was," closely parallel the prodigal son's abasement to his father: "I am no more worthy to be called thy son." Both men, young and old, feel shame at their old selves. Both emerge from their experience marvelously renewed. Scrooge becomes wholly and healthfully re-committed to the world he used to address with his signature rebuke, "Bah, humbug!" His new, very nearly reborn, self amazes him: "I'm a baby. Never mind. I don't care." His rebirth is healthfully "care-less."

Scrooge is filled with generous wonder at even the most (literally) pedestrian street doings. Scrooge leans out his window and hails a random kid in the street below. The old man asks whether the lad knows the "poulterer's in the next street but one?" The lad does—no surprise; but the previously un-neighborly, now newly reformed Scrooge considers it a wonder. The quotidian has become miraculous. He calls him "a delightful boy," and exults, "it's a pleasure to talk to him!" It is one of Dickens' most astute psychological touches.

The former miser then proceeds to tip the lad and commissions him to buy the huge turkey he will send to the Cratchits. Both stories thus confirm the personal renewals with a feast, a fundamental Christian motif for the renewal of community. Both declare the Christian message in its purest, most psychologically redemptive form. The prodigal's father's implicit sadness at his son's departure in the gospel parable is transformed at the end by joy at his return. Scrooge's former bitterness similarly yields to uncritical, generous love. These two specimens of what I am terming "fictional religion"—Christ's (Luke's, at least) and Dickens'—both deliver psychological insights into the value of self-criticism. They offer as well a profound and central Christian exhortation: to be open to redemptive experience, to "let go and let God."

Most crucially, both are the products of literary imaginations working on, and turning into a vivid narrative, a received Christian truth. Both carry on the process observed by Robert Alter about "the makers of biblical narrative." His subject was the Old Testament creative artists, but it applies to our pair as well. "They were moved to work out their vision of human nature and history...in prose fiction...in the manipulation of which they took delight" (156). The success of these two writers is self-evident. Luke's after all, made it into the Bible! And Dickens' secular tale has assumed very nearly divine status as an embodiment of the Christian message—well, at least the Christmas spirit. His tale revived for modern ears and hearts the holiday celebration whose foundation was laid in the birth narratives crafted by Luke and Matthew.

This experimental pairing makes the case that literary works, even those composed for a secular audience, can reach for, discover, and transmit profound insights into the human condition, insights as poignant and definitive as those created with an explicit theological and missionary agenda. The fictional, the invented, can be as inspired (and inspiring) as what we have been brought up to call "Scripture."

This Book's Mission

My purpose is far less presumptuous than it may sound. I think it confers a double benefit. True, I may be challenging believers to take a more rational, more scholarly, more historical-critical approach to what many ages have agreed to consider sacred, possibly even writ in stone. We continue to defer to the definition of what was to be considered Holy, imposed by a conclave of fourth-century bishops. But an honest assessment, putting our God-given reason to work, can yield splendid benefits. And what's more, I will compensate for what some might consider a deprivation by freeing up a far larger array of divine inspiration. Literary creators and their creations, from those of Chaucer to those of C. S. Lewis, are every bit as inspired *and* inspirational as the canonical texts of the Bible. In so doing, I am reaching out to a wider audience now arising, a "people who," Dewey observes, "couple their religious quest with intelligent discourse" (2008). An examination of the dozen writers I have chosen will allow us to see how thoughtful artists over the last half a millennium have taken the Christian doctrine they have inherited and applied its tenets and spirit to the intellectual needs, social contexts, and cultural biases of their age. Exploring these works, therefore, yields not only fresh doctrinal insights but a glimpse into the values and worldviews of the eras that gave birth to them. It yields as well—here the English teacher in me makes an appearance—a deeper appreciation of each man's literary craft.

Dewey calls for "the best minds and imaginations [to come] to the table" (2010). I join that anticipated feast, confessing that I lack the Westar Institute members' collective theological knowledge and judgment. But I offer a comparable expertise. I hope to broaden the Westar Institute's scope by bringing into its sacred premises a common-law, or at least deeply affectionate, sister discipline—literary criticism.

Works Cited

Alter, Robert. *The Art of Biblical Narrative.* New York: Basic Books, 1981.

Dewey, Arthur. Editorial. *The Fourth R* 21,3 (May/June 2008), p. 2.

——. Editorial. *The Fourth R* 22,4 (July/August 2009), p. 2.

——. Editorial. *The Fourth R* 23,3 (July/August 2010), p. 4.

1

Geoffrey Chaucer

Late Medieval Orthodoxy

G eoffrey Chaucer is far too humane and far too wise
to be too strict a doctrinal constructionist: he is, after
all, a poet. Yet he is perhaps the most orthodox proponent
of Christian doctrine among the writers we will encounter,
particularly in the one "Canterbury Tale" we will explore—
that of the Wife of Bath. Chaucer was writing in the late
fourteenth century, a time when European Christianity
was, in spite of strong "protesting" pressures, still unified.
The Gutenberg Bible lay a half century in the future, that
technological marvel which would encourage folks to start
prying doctrine out of the hands of clerics and formulate
their own thoughts about Scripture. Martin Luther would
not post his 95 revolutionary and anti-institutional Theses
for more than a century; Thomas Jefferson's heavily re-
dacted bible lay four centuries in the future; the Westar
Institute and the Jesus Seminar, five.

It is nonetheless undeniable that the poet's portraits of
the travelers to Canterbury include a wide variety of corrupt and sinful characters, and that several of the most
egregious are church officials. The character and behavior of men like the monk, the pardoner, and the sum-
moner would provide more than ample ammunition for
later Church reformers. Though Chaucer's faith is deeply
traditional, his awareness of and contempt for these corrupt figures makes him a genuine if early Renaissance hu-
manist. His belief system seems orthodox, but his spirit is
extraordinarily humane. He delights in the intimate and

precise capture of human characters, whether virtuous (rare) or fallible (far more usual).

He is also quite a literary revolutionary in his effort to reproduce—in minute details of gesture, voice, and clothing—the inhabitants of the world through which he moved. These 29 Canterbury pilgrims (well, 30 if one counts Chaucer himself; that's part of the *Tales'* realism) represent all classes and a wide swath of professions in the England of 1390, from cook to haberdasher to merchant to knight to (yes) poet, along with the wide swath of churchmen.

Chaucer's brilliant narrative tapestry is above all realistic; it introduces his readers to a variety of purportedly actual characters at a real place and time. Indeed, as we commence our literary walk, we should note that Christian literature, perhaps in subconscious tribute to the faith's founder, seems eager to focus its attention on the common, everyday men and women of the world. Chaucer creates a framework for his tales that is grounded in the everyday milieu of contemporary London and England much as Shakespeare wrote for the popular theatre, not the nobility, and Dickens sought to entertain the middle masses who were growing in both size, and literary appreciation.

The Wife of
Bath's Tale

Chaucer's aim, though, is more profound than mere realism. He sets his diverse pilgrims' interactions at a particularly symbolic time of year: springtime. As his famous "General Prologue" puts it,

> What that Aprill with his shoures soote [sweet]
> The droghte of March hath perced to the roote
> And bathed every veyne in swich liquor
> Of which vertu engendred is the flour...
> Than longen folks to goon on pilgrimage. (1–4, 12)

Spring is the season when the natural world revives; its very roots are soaked in water the unique virtue ("vertu," or essence) of which is to create flowers, to revive life. So, too, for people: some are motivated to visit Canterbury. Their honest faith prompts them to make the trek in gratitude for Saint Thomas a Becket, "the holy blissful martir," who has helped them "whan that they ware seeke [ill]" (17–18). But there is another group of folks, still with us, who are prompted by other urges, like sexual desire or the purely human longing to travel and mingle. Spring brings those desires back to life. Chaucer brilliantly captures both human impulses—the longing for the transcendent side by side with the longings of the flesh.

The narrative framework for this proto-documentary portrait of England is provided by the pilgrims' host, Harry Bailley, the owner of the Tabard Inn. He offers a plan for both the journey and the story-telling. To make the long trek to Canterbury more bearable, each pilgrim will tell two tales en route and two on the return journey. Whoever in Bailley's judgment tells the best tale will earn a meal upon the pilgrims' return, "at oure aller cost." He also announces the two criteria vital to capturing that prize: the winning story must offer "best sentence and moost solaas." It must both teach and entertain its listeners. The newly-formed community of pilgrims acquiesces in Bailley's plan and agree "that he wolde been our governour/And oure tales juge" (813–14). They all agree to contribute to the eventual feast, which at journey's end will thereby celebrate fellowship, moral education, and the pleasures of fiction. Fellowship will be a crucial concept throughout the stories examined in this book.

The "Wyf of Bathe," who tells the story, is clearly a creature more of flesh than faith. She loves life and she especially loves men's attention. Nor is this her first holy pilgrimage. She has been married five times and is on

the prowl for a sixth mate. Her literary creator has lav-
ished many remarkable techniques of characterization
on her; one of them is to assign physical attributes which
reflect an inner, spiritual flaw. That she is "somdeel deef"
(446), for example, is an outward and visible sign of her
mental obtuseness and physical self-indulgence. She has
trouble both in comprehending others' words and God's
Word.

To understand the wife and to see how the tale she tells
also reveals her nature, it is useful to glance at the long
"Prologue" to that tale. There we learn that the one doctrine to which she owes chief allegiance is "Experience."
It is indeed the very first word out of her mouth, and she
insists she would follow its revelations, even "though noon
auctoritee/Were in this world,"—that is, even if there were
no other source of wisdom or guidance available ("Wife
of Bath's Prologue," 1–2). She announces—and this is
what makes her so contemporary and believable a character—that she lets her lived life define her values and *mo-
res*, with no reference to received wisdom, even Christian
doctrine. But the irony is that the story she tells, ostensibly a fairy-tale set in Arthurian times, is straight Christian
doctrine. With his typically genial irony, Chaucer shows
us how wholly the wife misjudges and misreads the lesson
of Christian humility and obedience which is, as we will
see, her story's moral. Like Milton's Eve, another woman
who will praise experience explicitly and fulsomely, this
determined woman turns her back on the wide range of
wisdom and authority available to her.

That long prologue also offers a fine example of this
knowledgeable ignorance in the way she assesses her indulgent lifestyle. She brags that whenever she went "on these
pilgrimages" (her husband was usually away in London at
the time), she always wore fancy scarlet clothes and never

had to worry about worms or rust spoiling them "for they were used weel" (562). Give her credit at least for knowing Jesus' "auctoritee"—"lay not up treasure for yourself on earth where moth and rust do corrupt" would be the King James version two centuries later—though she employs it in precisely the wrong way. *Her* treasure is in constant use; it is continually invested, not laid up (set aside), for the purposes of sex. And, for her, sex is a means to several worldly ends—a good time, a new husband, and greater wealth. She thinks only of the present, and her pleasure in so doing drives away any possible concern with, or willingness to contemplate, deeper spiritual values.

Her commitment to indulgence makes her deaf to her Savior's moral advice. Chaucer even goes so far as to have her cite Jesus' specific words to the Samaritan woman, the woman who, like her, has had five husbands. "…you have had five husbands, and the one whom you now have is not your husband; in that you spoke truly" (John 4:18). The reader expects the wife will make the connection and perhaps apply it to herself, but in the next breath she dashes those expectations: "What that He mente thereby that I kan not sayn" ("Prologue," 20). Her deafness to Scripture is profound. Her reliance on sheer, indulgent experience makes its injunctions incomprehensible.

Chaucer here is brilliant. By showing the wife's distance from the advice she quotes, the poet actually confirms the legitimacy of those New Testament doctrines. At the same time, her lack of comprehension is so total that she emerges as a delightfully credible (all-too-human) sinner. Her choice of story, and her interpretation of it, are further subtle devices for characterizing her. It's one of the many pleasures of reading Chaucer that the person telling the tale doesn't get it, either in the story or her own life. But we do. Chaucer has it both ways: he reaffirms

Christian teaching while bringing to vivid life a believably fallen human being.

The plot of the "Tale" is simple. One of King Arthur's young knights is out riding and comes upon a maiden. He rapes her. The penalty for such a crime in Arthur's noble conclave is death, but his Queen intercedes and asks her husband for permission to try the criminal. It's the first of many instances in the story of a man yielding to a woman. Our flawed narrator, the Wife, is incapable of nice intellectual discrimination; she mistakes Arthur's chivalrous gesture as merely another valuable instance of female empowerment.

She fails to see it as an instance of marital harmony, perhaps because that is an "experience" she has rarely enjoyed. We see clearly that Arthur is bending the set legal procedure out of deference to his wife's wise judgment. The queen may well see the moment as an educational opportunity for the "lusty bachelor." She offers an alternate mercy to temper the king's "letter-of-the-law, Old Testament" justice. And so it proves. But the wife who tells the story is immune to such theological sophistication. She reads her sensibility and her priorities into everything.

The queen decrees that the knight be granted the formulaic "year and a day" to search the world and find out the answer to a vital question: "What is it that women most desire?" Having performed an abhorrent act, perhaps he can devote a humble year to acquiring a moral education. During that potentially life-saving quest he hears any number of answers—high status, good sex, wealth, flattery. The night before his return to court, the knight encounters a ring of dancing fairies, which evaporates, leaving an old woman. Long story short, she gives him the answer: authority ("Wommen desyren to have sovereyntee.../over hir housbond"; "Wife's Tale," 182–83). Her only condition is that, if her answer saves his life, he must grant her first wish.

Sure enough, the court next day concurs with his solution. Whereupon, no surprise, the old woman arises and makes her request: marriage. The last thing such a young and gallant fellow as he would wish is to be forced into a union with such a hag. That disgust, though, sets the stage for the story's powerful, and deeply religious, climax and lesson. In bed on their honeymoon night, she makes a convincing ethical observation as well as a profound reminder of the knightly obligations he is still disregarding:

> "Is this the lawe of King Arthures hous?
> …I am your owene love and eek your wyf;
> I am she which hath saved your lyf." (233–36)

Clearly, the ungrateful knight still needs some serious moral reform. The rapist's year of searching has taught him nothing about proper moral deportment. Episcopal Bishop John Shelby Spong reminds us that Jesus "understood that sexist prejudice warps the man and diminishes his humanity," (259). The knight is proof of that acutely Christ-like insight. But it is his new wife who will soon set him right. She will do so through an appeal to Jesus as the ideal role model of *both* behavior *and* values. That appeal's deep significance is clear from the particular theological allusion she makes. Responding to his distaste for her, she coolly announces that "I coude amende al this/…Er it were days thre" (250–52). That three-day allusion hints at an imminent resurrection, one that will prove moral for him, physical for her.

Good educator that she is, the hag starts by asking him to identify the reasons he is upset. He complies: "Thou art so loothly and so old also,/And thereto comen of so lowe a kind" (242–43). In short, she's ugly, old, and low-class. While the men amongst us might sympathize with his plight, we would be making as superficial a judgment as he. The new wife's subsequent homily is intended to get him to see past her loathsome externals and achieve a deeper spiritual understanding.

His objections declared, she thereupon launches into a lengthy, traditional, and authentically Christian homily. She turns out to be a living repository of both worldly wisdom and New Testament doctrine, and she takes him to task for each of those three superficial judgments. She begins her homily by rejecting his definition of "class," citing the key point that "Crist wol we clayme of him our gentillesse" (261); living by Christ's moral standards, as enunciated in Holy Scripture, is the surest key to and truest source of, gentility. Further,

> Thy gentillese cometh fro God alone;
> Than comth our verray gentillesse of grace,
> It was no thing biquethe us with our place. (306–8)

You cannot inherit moral stature with your social status, she says. Such status is a product of God's grace. So it's time, young man, for some prayerful humility.

She next ties class to poverty. Once again, Christ provides the unassailable antidote to the knight's poor judgment. Jesus lived his life in poverty and certainly would never choose a "vicious" (vice-ridden) course of life. She spends most of her intimate sermon on this key spiritual issue, but goes on to cover the other two. She is old? Well, we usually associate old age with wisdom, especially in men (355). No cause for rejecting her there (though it is another subtle feminist jibe: "Give us women the same respect you grant old men"). He just needs to expand his field of vision. As for her looks, she reminds him that her bad looks guarantee that...well, he need never fear her being unfaithful. Since no one else would want her, she will never stray.

Having delivered this firm spiritual lesson, she now offers him a worldly deal. It's a chance to test out whether her spiritual lecture can be—in the words of a splendid Anglican collect for Advent—marked, learned, inwardly digested, and put into effect. Whether, in a sense, the individual moral kingdom she has offered him may "come" on his "earth". Here's her offer: he may have her young and beautiful (there's that fairytale motif again) but be unsure of her loyalty; or he may keep her old and count on her faithfulness. His decision confirms the success of the moral education she has imparted: he now calls her "My lady and my love, and my wyf so dere" and lets her decide. "I put me in your wyse governance" (374–75). And, miracle of miracles, that new spiritual humility earns him a fleshly marvel. She transforms (like the worldly Papageno's hag of a wife in Mozart's fairytale opera *The Magic Flute*) into what we moderns might term a "babe." Not only does she blossom magically ("she was so fair and so yong therto") but he gains a second benefit: faithfulness. "And she obeyed him in every thing/That mighte doon him plesance or lyking" (399–400).

The story confirms the traditional Christian paradox that by losing, by yielding authority to a moral superior, one gains. To serve God is to enjoy perfect freedom. (This motif will return with the Anglican priest George Herbert in his poem "The Collar.") The narrative the Wife relates is an effective sermon on a traditional Christian teaching, as true to the gospel message as are the gospels themselves. It's all fiction of course (in fact, it's a fictional tale told by a fictional character in a made-up story of traveling pilgrims), but there are also, as we are learning from modern biblical scholarship, many fictional or poetic elements in those first four gospels. Chaucer's fictional exposition of religious doctrine packs a remarkable theological wallop.

Still, Chaucer shows his incisive psychological sophistication by showing how that narrator, the Wyf, is characteristically deaf to the very message her story has trumpeted.
She emerges none the wiser, as we see in her summative
demand that "Jesu Crist us sende/Housbonds meke,
yonge, and fresshe abedde" (402–3). The woman who tells
the story, of course, thinks in terms of winning for herself
a similar benefit of physical renewal. She fails to grasp that
the woman in the story is the voice of Christ. She sees the
message as one of power, not humility. She wants control,
and she wants nightly sexual pleasure. She is every bit as
acquisitive and indulgent as she was before she began her
tale.

The most telling sign of her failure to grasp her tale's
"sentence" is that she longs for "grace t'overbyde hem that
we wedde" (404)—to outlive each husband and inherit
his goods and property. That narcissistic grace for which
she prays (it sounds more like a demand) is far removed
from the spiritual self-denial urged by the hag in her tale,
that special "grace…that cometh fro God alone." I'd go
further. I think the Wife's tale is one of wish fulfillment.
Approaching middle age herself, she longs, deep down,
for the sort of physical renewal the old hag achieves. She
misreads the Christian homilist in her tale not as a model
of self-denial, but as a proposed life of material, sexual,
and marital acquisition.

Works Cited

Chaucer, Geoffrey. *The Canterbury Tales*. Ed. A. Kent and
    Constance Haieatt. New York: Bantam, 1964.
Spong, Shelby John. *Jesus for the Non-Religious*. New York:
    HarperOne, 2007.

2

William Shakespeare's *Macbeth*

A Vision of a Godly Kingdom

As New Testament scholarship explores more deeply into the historical Jesus, we can see that many works of literary fiction are probably untrue to the vision the man actually voiced. Still, we see that these works of art are remarkably persuasive imaginings of what over the centuries *grew into* the officially-proclaimed Christian ideals. Such artists as Chaucer, Herbert, and Dickens have done yeoman service in adapting and re-visioning for their particular eras those doctrinal insights that the church began proclaiming as fixed and final during the faith's early centuries.

One point that today's scholars are coming to see is that at the heart of Jesus of Nazareth's mission lay a profound but never definitively articulated notion of God's kingdom, a term the Jesus Seminar translates as His "imperial rule." As Dominic Crossan, among others, has pointed out, Christ was offering to his disciples, whom Crossan calls his "companions," a vision of the kingdom that quite explicitly was *not* one in *overt* political competition with the Roman powers that be. It was, instead, an internally-ordered dedication to God's word through a determined commitment to a godly life of mercy and justice. The nature of that glorious realm is one that, perhaps for safety's sake, Jesus shadowed darkly in his parables. That alternative order is hinted parabolically, or by only implicit contrast. Marcus Borg has suggested that Jesus' notion of "the Kingdom of God referred to what life on earth would be like if God were king and the kingdoms of this world, the domination systems of this world, were not" (187).

Those who had ears, of course, could piece the vision together. In its very simplicity, that vision is a radical one—a return to the root (*radix* in Latin) of Judaic belief: Love of God and love of neighbor. As Jesus said to a lawyer who asked him how to live, "You shall love the Lord Your God with all your heart, and with all your soul, and with all your mind. This is the great and first commandment. And the second is like unto it, You shall love your neighbor as yourself" (Matthew 22:38–40). It is as simple as Micah's powerfully eloquent, "And what does the Lord require of you? To act justly, to love mercy, and to walk humbly with your God" (6:8). Prophets always spoke things simply, boiled down to their essentials. Though Jesus clothed his spiritual advice in parables, it is nonetheless clear, based on the consequences, that both the Roman and Jewish authorities recognized the danger his simple vision posed. He voiced an inconvenient truth, as we might say today.

The work of art that, to my mind, most fully captures and projects as a viable possibility Borg's godly commonwealth is *Macbeth*. In it, Shakespeare suggests the requisite elements of one such godly kingdom—the outlines, obligations, and benefits of a genuinely Christian commonwealth. Of course, the culture for which the playwright was evoking such a realm was a firmly patriarchal one, and thus markedly different from the one Jesus was recommending. After all, Shakespeare is, in effect, celebrating the successful achievement of a Christian realm that Jesus proposed only in parables, while Rome was self-evidently at odds with the faith Jesus was proposing.

In Shakespeare's day, all the members, from king to nobleman to serf, owed the same allegiances. The *imperium* they agreed to reverence *was* Christian. More than that, *Macbeth* was staged to honor England's new king,

James I (James VI of Scotland), the man who'd also just become the new patron of the playwright's acting troupe, known under Queen Elizabeth as the Lord Chamberlain's Men and under James as The King's Men. I think it is fair to assume, then, that the Bard in his drama of welcome is suggesting to his new boss the requisite elements of a godly kingdom, suitably re-imagined for the actual, live British realm he was inheriting. Clearly a powerful drama in its own right, *Macbeth* is a set of voiced and enacted recommendations to the new king of what a Christian realm might look like.

The play, one of Shakespeare's most poetically rich, opens as a tale of rebellion, though that rebellion is kept off-stage and described only by report. A Scottish lord (the Thane of Cawdor) has taken arms against the good king Duncan, with aid lent by the King of Norway. The rebellion is quickly put down, valiantly suppressed by Duncan's brave and loyal noblemen, the "thanes" Macbeth and Banquo. As they journey back to receive his thanks, they meet three witches (agents of evil, a far cry from the "good" hag who appears to Chaucer's knight). They prophesy that Macbeth shall be king and that Banquo, though never king himself, will father a line of kings. Macbeth's instant and instinctive response to the implied assassination of Duncan demonstrates his profound sense of duty: that "suggestion['s] horrid image doth unfix my hair/And make my seated heart knock at my ribs/Against the use of nature" (I.iii.135–37). This fundamentally moral man recognizes that seeking to murder his king is an unnatural deed; it goes against the "fixed," "seated," and organic order of things, whether in the body or the body politic. One's body is at one with the wider commonwealth.

Macbeth's grievous inner conflict between ambition and obedience in fact makes up the remainder of the play. Macbeth resists, his wife persuades, and eventually he is seduced by her into murdering Duncan, an assassination that takes place at his own home and castle. In the next chapter, we will see that George Herbert's man of God, in "The Collar," undergoes a similarly intense inner battle; his, though, will last a matter of minutes. Macbeth's becomes the essential drama of the entire two-hour play. If Macbeth could rely solely on his own moral conscience, he could perhaps withstand his temptation. But his own all-too-human ambition paired with his all-too-ambitious wife proves irresistible. The unwilling assassin is soon dragged into dealing with his vicious deed's external-military and inward-psychological consequences. Those challenges take up the remainder of the play.

—◦—

Macbeth wrestles with his guilt but attains a certain nobility in admitting it and coming to terms with it. His wife, on the other hand, having suppressed her natural sense of morality, out of both marital and personal ambition, goes mad with delayed guilt. In the end, the good Scots rise up, Duncan's legitimate heir Malcolm is lent aid by the saintly English king, and their combined armies capture the tyrant's castle and behead him.

The play's moral focus, that long internal debate, is most evident when Macbeth returns to his castle, the crucial setting. Prior to Duncan's arrival, Lady Macbeth receives her husband's letter reporting the witches' prophecy; knowing him as she does, she worries that he "has too much of the milk of human kindness" in him to do the deed (I.v.17). That is an important image. Milk, of course, is healthful. And the word "kindness" in Shakespeare's time meant "fellow feeling," or communal comradeship. (We get the word "kin" from it.) These notions tie to the whole system of images Shakespeare employs to give us a sense of a normally healthful, organic, and natural system of values. It defines the playwright's conception of a godly kingdom. Milk, health, nourishment, and fellowship constitute its beating heart.

The requisite ceremonial expression of love to the lord of such a realm is not, the playwright suggests, a personal burden or chore; it is, rather, an expression of gratitude for the secure communal order that ruler guarantees. We see this when Lady Macbeth welcomes Duncan to Glamis. He thanks her for the required ceremonial gesture, though he knows it is a double imposition—a chore for her as welcoming hostess and a burden for him, who must reciprocate by receiving her welcome graciously:

> The love that follows us sometime is our trouble
> Which still we thank as love. Herein I teach you
> How you shall bid God 'ild [reward] us for your pains
> And thank us for your trouble. (I.vi.11–14)

My appreciation of your offer inspires you in turn to thank God for making you make that effort. The complex weaving of "you," "your," and "us" makes the harmonious point. The commonwealth is continually interactive and inter-dependent. The whole order, with God at its center, rejoices at the very obligations demanded of it. The exchange might also be seen as a profound piece of Christian doctrine tied to Jesus' Matthean command about loving one's enemies. The psychological burden thereby demanded is at the heart of self-denying, godly charity. One trains one's mind and spirit to reject the convenient and do the psychologically difficult. In so doing, society, nation, and self mutually benefit.

Macbeth repeats the insight later when he observes that "the labor we delight in physics pain" (II.iii.49). The reverence for the figure at the center of the political order is a reassuring reminder of how sacred that order is. As the knight in Chaucer's tale learned, and as Herbert's priest will, a humane and sacred order rewards one for suspending one's personal independence and yielding obedience to a superior. For the knight, the reward is a recognition of his new wife's articulate Christian wisdom; for Herbert's priest, it is a previously-learned obedience now restored to health. Both men experience the redemptive paradox of proper service. Macbeth voices and believes it early on; his Lady, however, merely mouths it.

Indeed, Shakespeare threads the play with a rich abundance of such imagery, words that recur and spell out a complex range of elements in that beneficent order. One of them is Nature. Nature is both beneficent and procreative. Its role in the play's ideal vision is commemorated most memorably in Banquo's paean to Macbeth's castle, which unites birds, air, and masonry: He observes "the temple-haunting martlet" whose "pregnant" nests confirm the presence of "delicate air," which "smells wooingly here." The images combine to synthesize religion (the "temple"), procreation and fertility ("pregnant"), and courtship ("wooingly") in a celebration of sensual delight. That the owners of the place lurk within those walls, plotting murder, does not detract from the legitimacy of the vision Banquo beholds and proclaims (I.vi.4–10). Add to those elements the king. He stands at the order's center, like a loving father, which incorporates another dimension: familial relationships. Lady Macbeth, in an early warning of the psychic turmoil that will eventually destroy her mental health, confesses the king's paternal role: "Had [Duncan] not resembled my father as he slept I'd done the deed myself" (II.ii.12–13).

Shakespeare goes yet further. He weaves in two additional ideas that deserve even more careful scrutiny: feasting and separation. *Feasting* fuses the idea of nourishment with notions of community and celebration; these ideas get ample presentation while Macbeth's actions in fact separate him—*exclude* him further and further—from that restorative order.

Close to the play's conceptual heart, feasting and re-storative meals are a key metaphor for the healthful order Shakespeare is recommending. We see it early on, when Duncan praises Macbeth's loyal valor with an unusual metaphor: "In his commendations I am fed;/It is a banquet to me" (I.iv.55–56). Acts of loyalty to the crown, along with the praise they earn, nourish the king, just like those ceremonious welcomes he must endure. It is he who stands at the heart of the order; that order's members sacrifice personal ambition—even their very lives—for the commonweal. To serve the king loyally is to offer him psychic food and nourishment; the act is as nutritional to the order as milk.

Most usefully for our purposes, the idea of a feast also puts us in mind of Jesus, to whose ministry communal meals were central. The earliest New Testament accounts are rife with moments at table. The Pharisees even accuse the upstart preacher of supping with far too many people, especially those of the wrong sort. Healthful communing is, thus, at the center of the Christian message and, as such, it recurs frequently. At the conclusion of his ministry, in what I take to be a later literary addition inserted to further an early agenda of the church, Jesus enjoins Peter to "feed my sheep" (John 21:17), and today most Christians still enact the Last Supper weekly as a ceremonial "memorial" to his last communal meal. Borg recognizes that the "sacrament of bread and wine...is manifestly a post-Easter development. Yet it has its roots in the pre-Easter meal practice of Jesus" (157). No coincidence, Shakespeare inserts such a healthful and communal ceremony into the very heart of the Christian kingdom proposed by his drama; Shakespeare's purpose, though, is more poetic, political, and moral than it is theological. In this sense, the word "banquet" is all the more resonant as a pun on Banquo's name; the historical Banquo was the

Scottish ancestor of the new King James. The playwright is thereby paying a compliment to his new employer's regal forefather. The actual banquet on the stage is simultaneously a living, graceful tribute.

The banquet scene in Act III lies truly at the play's center in both timing and theme. A banquet, of course, provides sustaining food, but more crucial is its ceremonial import. At a crucial moment, Lady Macbeth upbraids her newly-crowned husband: "You do not keep the feast," a phrase Anglicans still employ for weekly Eucharistic meals:

> The feast is sold
> That is not often vouch'd, while 'tis a-making,
> 'Tis given with welcome: to feed were best at home;
> From thence, the sauce to meat is ceremony;
> Meeting were bare without it. (III.iv.32–36)

Point number one: a feast is no feast, is not genuinely communal, unless members are made to feel welcome. Ritual ("ceremony") is crucial. Otherwise that common meal is "sold;" it serves to separate provider and guest. More: Shakespeare employs a brilliant pun that proclaims the intimate connection between "meat" (food, sustenance, replenishment) and community ("meeting"). The two are mutually reinforcing. A gathering sustains, while "to feed" is the act of a selfish, private, disconnected individual. William Faulkner will set "Barn Burning's" opening trial in a country general store, where the community gathers for both its bodily and jurisprudential sustenance. It's a communal ideal revered by both artists. We will return to Shakespeare's masterful handling of this particular banquet a little later.

Divorce and Separation

Such an ideal world is one from which it is hard to imagine anyone excluding him- or herself, above all the loyal and valiant Macbeth. As he and his Lady contemplate regicide, he answers his wife's accusation of cowardice with the insistence that "I dare do all that may become a man./Who dares do more is none" (I.vii.46–47). He has a firm sense of moral order and fitness; he knows from the start that his contemplated deed will remove him from that blissful, healthful polity. He knows where he belongs. In a final summing up of how far he has fallen from the ideal of a communal feast, Macbeth laments, "I have supped full with horrors." *His* feasting, by virtue of his own evil moral choices, has been horrific. It has also been experienced alone.

It does not take away from the legitimacy of that ideal realm that the play dramatizes how far one man (urged on by one woman) has departed from it. Their fall does not disqualify the proposed ideal, any more than the wife of Bath's misunderstanding of scripture renders the gospels invalid. On the contrary, Macbeth's pained and clear-eyed awareness of his evil at every stage in fact serves to confirm that order's legitimacy. For one thing, the play itself opens with a rebellion against Duncan—treason, both foreign and domestic. Nor does Macbeth's horrifying journey into regicide and its consequences disqualify the proposed ideal—it simply reminds us of the difficulty of achieving it. And what prevents its achievement is a very traditional theological concept: Original Sin. Macbeth and his wife both fall prey to it—the seductive power of our inner, natural, fallen selves, what Hamlet calls "our old stock" which, he reminds Ophelia, "You cannot so inoculate... but we shall relish of it" (*Hamlet,* III.i.117–19).

Shakespeare is a superlative poet, but he is also no stranger to stagecraft. He is the supreme *dramatic* poet of the British tradition. He makes his usual expert use of the stage to *visualize* Macbeth's successive steps of separation, his progressive divorce from that festive healthful community which the imagery of the play has proposed and celebrated. It begins the moment the witches' prophecy is confirmed by the king's messengers. When he hears of his promotion to Thane of Cawdor (a reward which confirms the witches' prediction), he drifts away, across the stage from them, and begins a lengthy *and private* soliloquy. Banquo notices his distance and self-involvement: "Look how our partner's rapt" (I.iii.142). That moment is a visible marker for the start of Macbeth's separation from the ideal order for which he so recently risked life and limb. Here he begins the internal moral debate that will detach himself from that healthful "partnership."

The closer he comes to doing the deed, the more physically removed from his fellows Macbeth becomes. The evening Duncan arrives at Macbeth's castle, a feast (another banquet) is given in his honor. But Macbeth's wife finds her husband, no longer a festive participant, lurking in the hallway outside the banquet chamber. As the scene begins, the playwright's explicit stage directions call for "a [butler] and divers servants with dishes and service over the stage." Shakespeare is here taking specific dramaturgical pains to visualize the sumptuous meal, the feast that is passing Macbeth by. His absence from it is symbolically telling. His lady upbraids him: "He has almost supped. Why have you left the chamber?" (I.vii. 29). She does not realize that, even this late, he is still wrestling with his conscience. His astonishingly chaotic soliloquy, as he foresees the universal outcry that will greet the murder, shows the disorder of the human mind and self when it unmoors itself from its proper place. He foresees that

> Pity, like a naked new born babe
> Striding the blast, or heaven's cherubim, horsed
> Upon the sightless couriers of the air
> Shall blow the deed in every eye
> That tears shall drown the wind. (I.vii.21–25)

The train of images displays the wanderings of an anticipatorily guilty mind.

The most poignant confirmation of Macbeth's divorce is also the most explicitly Christian. In reporting the incident later to his wife, he paints for her and us the moment he entered Duncan's chamber to murder him. He heard the king's grooms saying their prayers, and he found he could not participate. "One cried 'God bless us' and 'Amen' the other," but "I could not say 'Amen' when they did say 'God bless us.'" That social and ritual exclusion grows into an obsession even as he recollects it. Knowing the moral order far more deeply than his wife, Macbeth cannot help recurring to that frightening moment: "But wherefore could I not say 'Amen'? I had most need of blessing" (II.ii.28–30). His wife, characteristically, urges him to "Consider it not so deeply." Like Chaucer's knight on his wedding night, she is distressingly shallow, confident that "a little water clears us of this deed" (II.ii.64). She cannot begin to appreciate the horror of the separation her husband feels until later, when, in her madness, she constantly washes her hands, seeking far too late to cleanse herself of the act she encouraged. In this moment, however, her husband knows better. "No," he says, "this my hand/Will rather the seas incarnadine/ Making the green one red" (II.ii.58–60). He sees the cosmic import of his vile, life-quenching act. It will drench in blood the fertile, green world, and only when that green forest of Dunsinane advances upon his castle will Scotland's vital health be restored.

The most potent enactment of Macbeth's exclusion occurs in the play's central moment: that key banquet, the one he holds to celebrate his accession (III.iv). Not only is Macbeth determined, recalling the witches' prophecy, to keep his throne, but he has also hired assassins to slay both Banquo and his son, Fleance. In the banquet, the murdered Banquo literally lives up to his punning name. He'll participate in the new king's banquet. It is Banquo—his ghost, anyway—who takes his place at the

center of the table where all of Scotland's nobility is assembled. Shakespeare shows Macbeth trying and failing
thrice to take his seat "in the midst" (10) of the communal
feast. For one thing, he cannot join the noble fellowship
because he is repeatedly called away to get those assassins'
reports. Steps he must take to *keep his place* as king prevent
him from *taking his place* in the noble fellowship. Next,
it's only our eyes and Macbeth's conscience that can see
the ghost of Banquo. He enters and quite literally usurps
Macbeth's rightful place at the center of that festive table.
The new king's companions urge him to join them, but to
Macbeth's eyes it seems that "the table's full" (45). That
sight is a profound insight. That communal table of the
nation is indeed complete; he has been excluded, not just
physically but morally. Shut out from the "meeting," he is
deprived of the table's restorative "meat."

His resulting guilty, fearful rage breaks up the gathering "with most admir'd disorder" (109). The chaos simultaneously predicts and confirms that the tyrant's realm is
doomed. Indeed, Lady Macbeth tries to cover his rage and
fear by urging the guests to "feed and regard him not." As
we saw earlier, "To feed were best at home. From thence
the sauce to meat is ceremony." Macbeth has made such
ceremony impossible; each guest has become an individual feeder, no longer part of a communal feast. The entire
banquet scene shows Shakespeare's poetic, dramaturgical,
and intellectual powers working at white-hot heat.

Only the holy hand of England's good King Edward
II will bring Scotland back to concord. He has the king's
miraculous gift of healing leprosy, and it is a crucial gift
for, as Malcolm tells Macduff, "To the succeeding royalty
he leaves/The healing benediction" (IV.iii.172–73). Well,
James I is such a succeeding royal. The playwright hereby
reminds him that he will receive the sacred gift and with it
the obligation to continue that holy tradition. In *Macbeth*,

the king's curative gift adds yet another Christ-like, healing gift to the mix of overall beneficence soon to return to Scotland.

It is no surprise that, as Macbeth grows farther into his tyranny and makes his land a living hell, the doctor (a restorer of health) who comes to tend to Lady Macbeth proves powerless. The usurper's kingdom is past cure, both spiritual and bodily. Macbeth begs of him, "Canst thou not minister"—the verb suggests his services are almost priestly—"to a mind diseased? Pluck from the memory a rooted sorrow?" (V.iii.40). No, in this play the cure must come from without—only Malcolm, Duncan's rightful heir, blessed by the English king's holy touch, can effect that healing. The doctor reminds Macbeth, "Therein the patient must minister to himself" (45–46). Spiritual health is a matter of individual will and volition, and both king and queen have for far too long devoted their free will to evil and ambition.

Another particularly doctrinal moment occurs as Macbeth arms himself to prepare for his final battle. The name of his loyal servant is Seyton, probably pronounced "Satan." Shakespeare makes the nature of the evil king's commitment more than obvious. There is also an amusing moment when another servant enters to report that the forest is indeed moving. A sign both of his frustration and of how far he has lost that kindly milk is evident in his striking the man, calling him "thou cream-faced loon!" Having been drained of his natural milk, he dismisses the bad news, calling the reporter a member of the elite who look like cream.

In my doctoral dissertation forty years ago, I argued that this play is, in the most profound sense, a comedy. I still think so. Shakespeare's drama confirms the availability of a regenerative moral order, from which, once one strays, one is banished. Macbeth's pained but clear awareness, at every stage, that he is paying the price for his moral divorce merely confirms that order's power and permanence. Still, Shakespeare's genius is such that Macbeth's awareness of the consequences of his actions makes him a more sympathetic, even tragic, hero. The play is thus one of the most poignant and powerful expressions of the ideal of the healthful and loving kingdom first hinted at in Jesus' subtly voiced, imagined alternative to Rome's iron rule.

Works Cited

Borg, Marcus. *Jesus*. New York: HarperOne, 2006.

Shakespeare, William. *Hamlet*. Shakespeare Navigators. www.shakespeare-navigators.com

———. *Macbeth*. Shakespeare Navigators. www.shakespeare-navigators.com

3

George Herbert's
"The Collar" & John Donne's
"Holy Sonnet #14"

Anglican Agony

Some literature is poignant simply through its ability to capture and convey accurately a recognizable human emotion. It's a feature of literature that the great English critic Dr. Samuel Johnson calls "just representations of general nature." Occasionally, as in Shakespeare's soliloquies, we admire in addition the beautiful precision with which the actual operation and motions of the human mind are captured. We behold a beating brain. Both John Donne—an Anglican priest who ultimately became Dean of St. Paul's Cathedral—and George Herbert—a similarly literate but rural Anglican priest—are powerful exemplars of such poetic skill and sharp psychological insight.

They are also an intriguing pair, for one can see them as ecclesiastical descendants of the men who wrote the gospels. Naturally, the hierarchical structures within which these authors worked differed markedly. Luke, after all, was writing for a very young, barely organized "church," more likely a small faith community in its institutional infancy. He was present at the faith's creation and helped shape it. Donne and Herbert, on the other hand, were the servants of a church which, though recently split from Rome, still had something like fifteen centuries of accumulated practice and doctrine upon which to draw. Both could count on an audience of believing readers who shared their sense of a practicing spiritual and intellectual community.

In any event, Herbert's "The Collar" and Donne's "Holy Sonnet 14" focus more closely on the inner spiritual life and psychology of a sinful man, and less so on matters of dogma. The poems are deeply personal and frankly confessional; each captures the mind and intense emotions of a fallen man of faith, actively wrestling with temptation. One speaker finally succeeds; for the other, success is elusive.

Herbert's poem (see Appendix) is neither theological nor strictly doctrinal; the piety it dramatizes could as easily be Jewish or Islamic, male or female. Indeed the psychological process it dramatizes, first of rebellion against then of acquiescence to, authority is something to which all can relate. That's one reason "The Collar" is still read in the twenty-first century; it is deeply admired even by agnostics. It is a portrait of a man wrestling with the life his faith has demanded of him; it paints the inner conflict between the selfish and the selfless; it pictures a soul longing to engage with the alluring pleasures of the world but, at the end, subsiding into atonement—in the word's original sense, becoming "at one" with God. The speaker longs to be released from his onerous religious obligations, yet by the end he yields with concise but profound humility.

William Wordsworth called poetry "emotion recollected in tranquility." Herbert's poem recollects and seeks to reproduce an intensely emotional but momentary assertion of rebellious independence; the drama ends before any rational or tranquil processing of that emotion has begun. In its dramatic intensity it resembles a Shakespearean soliloquy. The speaker begins with an act of sharp impatience: "I struck the board and cried 'No more!/I will abroad!/What? shall I ever sigh and pine?...'" He begins to review the things his calling has forced him to relinquish. His life is one of continual, humble requests: "Shall I be still in suit?"—that is, must I always beg, like a powerless dependent? All he can recall, and what he seeks to escape, are endless, recurring days of abstract philosophical reasoning: "Leave thy cold dispute/Of what is fit, and not," he orders himself. That habit of abstract meditation has yielded him only unrewarding pain: "Have I no harvest but a thorn/To let me blood...?"

Herbert's words here evoke a monkish ascetic, a religious hermit. The poem's title, "The Collar," suggests he is a priest or, at the very least, someone chained to a life of unwanted obligations. Furthermore, the title contains a pun: "collar" is a homonym for a word for anger, "choler." The self he has tried to deny for years is now rising up in irate resentment. His frustration makes him determined to seek newer, greener pastures, a longing revealed in a series of pained rhetorical reflections: "Sure there was wine/Before my sighs did dry it; there was corn/Before my tears did drown it." Here, "corn" is the British term for grain; he is in effect longing for bread and wine. His complaint rises to a firm declaration of intent: "Away! take heed;/I will abroad./Call in thy death's-head there; tie up thy fears." He asserts his right to freedom: "He that forbears/To suit and serve his need,/Deserves his load." Before, he was always "suing" to God for favor and attention and approval. Now he decides simply to "suit" himself. His petulance and anger remind us of the spoiled and self-indulgent knight in the Wife of Bath's tale, caught on his wedding night in a trap of his own devising. While we may sympathize with both men's frustrations, we see that each needs to be cured of his narcissistic obsession.

And just at that instant comes the cure:

> But as I raved and grew more fierce and wild
>> At every word
> Methought I heard one calling *Child!*
>> And I replied, *My Lord.*

It takes Chaucer's old hag a three-page sermon to re-deem her new husband. Scrooge requires a long night of visitations by three spirits—two of them quite chatty. In Herbert, however, the instantaneous reform occurs in the newly-humble man's final two short syllables. His sub-mission confirms what the priest has always known, deep down. He owes full obedience to his "Lord." He sees in an instant that he has been indulging in a childish rage; he re-turns in an instant to the One whose service, his heart has long since recognized, *is* perfect freedom—freedom in spite of the occasional selfish, momentary slip.

The internal redemptive moment is as touching as the physical return of the prodigal son, a story no doubt original to Jesus but which that fine writer known as Luke turned into a powerful moral narrative. A major differ-ence, of course, is that here the potential prodigal, con-templating an indulgent life, entertains a vision that lasts maybe half a minute; it is not the product of several years' lived self-indulgence. Herbert, writing fifteen centuries af-ter Luke, mines the very Christian ethic of obedience that Luke was in truth instituting. In both, God the Father wel-comes home a wayward child. Yet again, a powerful work of art rivals, in its psychological force and poignancy, a message first announced in a gospel.

Donne (see Appendix) also employs the confessional, first-person pronoun throughout his sonnet, creating a comparably needy, emotionally distraught, speaker, who is a conventional sinful man longing intensely to return to God. His sonnet is also more doctrinally orthodox; its first line addresses a "three-personed God." The speaker does not, however, go on to pursue the theological implications of that invocation. He simply uses the term to suggest the triple power he hopes God can visit upon the erring man.

Each poem traces the effort of a man fighting for his independence. We see, in Herbert, a man committed to the religious calling, but longing for freedom; in Donne, a man engulfed in sin, longing for rescue. Indeed the sonnet's fourteen lines are a plea to God to release him from the sinful snares to which he has fallen prey. Herbert's takes only three short syllables ("Child"..."My Lord") to change rebellion into reconciliation. Donne instead analyzes his condition, showing an awareness of God's availability joined to a recognition that he is so far enmeshed in sin that his release will require far more. We do not know which particular deadly sin has captured him, whereas Herbert's is more explicit—a proud longing for independence declared by a man who has long felt ill-used. So far, for Donne's sinner, God has only "[knocked, breathed, shone and sought] to mend" him. These actions haven't been enough. He recognizes that the renewal he requires is so thorough-going that it can be expressed only through a paradox: "That I may rise and stand, o'erthrow me;" this, the first of several. The intensity it requires is expressed in some powerful alliterations—repeated "b" sounds—and enjambment: "Bend/Your force, to break, blow, burn, and make me new." The need is so intense that line three spills over into line four.

The speaker summons a series of metaphors to describe his entrapment with "Your enemy," whom we interpret, rather doctrinally, to be the Devil, though Donne never names him. The speaker compares himself to a medieval town that has been taken over ("usurped") by this evil force. It is as if he is the mayor of that captured town, who longs to let God in to its walls. I "labor to admit you." He continues the metaphor with an intriguing doctrinal point: "Reason, Your viceroy in me, me should defend." Here, he recognizes Reason as a gift from God, a substitute ("vice") "king" (from the French word, *roi*). Our capacity for rational thought is like a divine ambassador upon which we should rely to resist the Devil's allurements. But we lack the strength. Our reason is "captived" and has proven to be "weak or untrue." All too often we put our reason to the unworthy task of rationalizing. I'll start that diet tomorrow. I'll break off that affair next week. Incidentally, the assassin Macbeth made an interesting use of the idea of "reason." In explaining why he killed the grooms guarding King Duncan, he pretends that it was loyalty and valor that made him do it: "The expedition of my valiant love/Outrun the pauser, reason." Reason, calm thought, is a force of restraint, which Macbeth pretends was not strong enough to hold back his righteous anger at the grooms who, he pretends, killed the king. For Donne, it is a God-given protector.

In C. S. Lewis' children's tale, *The Voyage of the Dawn Treader* this moral phenomenon recurs (see chapter 9). Young Eustace Scrubb also learns, after being turned into a dragon as punishment for his narcissism, that our god-given powers are inadequate for reformation. We cannot redeem ourselves. No, we need God's direct—and painful—intervention; only He can rip off the lad's beastly scales. Donne likewise suggests that, because each fallible Christian ends up inevitably as evil's fiancé(e), God must do one of three things—"divorce" us from that enemy, "untie...that knot" if possible, or perhaps actually slice it through. The speaker is begging God to abrogate a sacrament; that apparently is the only way to dissolve the corrupt but all too natural marriage. To cleanse ourselves—this is where we see Donne at his most astonishingly daring and inventive—we need God not merely to imprison us, but to "ravish"—rape—us. Only by such abuse, which is more psychological or spiritual than sexual of course, may we hope to restore our moral chastity, our purity. The array of paradoxes startles us at first, but upon examination they reflect quite orthodox doctrine.

Indeed, as it so often does in religiously-inspired poems and literature, paradox lies at the heart of the poem's intellectual investigation. Chaucer's knight learned the redemptive paradox that service, yielding to a Christ-like moral superior, not only means freedom but also earns splendid rewards (and not only at bedtime). By yielding the control of the relationship to his wife, he earns—in worldly terms—a beautiful young woman, one who is loyal into the bargain. In doing so, the knight is yielding to moral directives of God's Son, which the old lady is merely reporting. So, too, for Donne. The speaker asks from God the kind of imprisonment that frees, the rape that purifies. Paradox, irony, and oxymoron all constitute the impossible union or juxtaposition of conceptual opposites. They all seek intellectually to put into words the ineffable nature of religious commitment.

Works Cited

Donne, John. "Holy Sonnet 14." P. 909 in *Norton Anthology of Literature*. Vol. 1. New York: Norton, 1968.

Herbert, George, "The Collar." P. 957 in *Norton Anthology of Literature*. Vol. 1. New York: Norton, 1968.

4

John Donne & Andrew Marvell

The Division between Body & Soul

It may still raise an eyebrow or two that John Donne, Dean of St. Paul's Cathedral, and crafter of marvelous sermons and profound spiritual meditations, also wrote vibrant love poems. Some of them are quite explicitly erotic. By the same token, Andrew Marvell is a master of love poetry, perhaps most memorably "To His Coy Mistress." But the seductive advice at the end of that poem to "Roll all our pleasures into one ball" in fact rests on deeply traditional conceptions. The speaker longs to "[have] space enough and time," but knows this is a pleasant but impossible hypothesis. He "hears time's chariot at [his] back;" he knows full well that the future will bring only an eternity that is deserted, empty and joyless. His romantic vision is, in short, grounded in traditional religious teaching; his most sublime love poem is based in strict religious doctrine. That the love poet can voice theology, and the Cathedral Dean write of love, speaks to the intellectual and artistic vitality at work in England in that fecund seventeenth century.

It was a deeply religious century; England and the Continent were each roiled in an enduring and often murderous argument over which version of Christian faith, Protestant or Catholic, was valid. These epic battles—the Continent's Thirty Years' War, England's Puritan revolt and subsequent beheading of King Charles—confirm that this was still an era of intense Christian religious belief. Only in the eighteenth century with the rise of the Enlightenment might it be said that a more rational examination of the tenets of Christianity began. Before then, there had been a nearly unspoken implicit trust in the received Christian doctrines that dominated serious artists' thoughts and guided their creations. These firm religious beliefs, in short, continued to undergird many creative and literary endeavors. Indeed, Marvell's friend and supporter John Milton, to whom we will turn in chapter 5, might be said to have brought a breath of fresh and creative Puritan air to the familiar literature of Genesis, retelling in brilliant and inventive fashion the entire story of the fall from a devoutly Protestant perspective. His majestic work, *Paradise Lost,* is proof of the vitality of religious faith still at work in English thought and literature.

The business of this chapter is to examine two further examples of the way religious thought could permeate the fabric of poetic work. The first is a love poem by Donne, "A Valediction Forbidding Mourning"; the second, "A Dialogue Between Soul and Body" by Andrew Marvell, takes explicit religious doctrine and creates a lively conversation (for both poems, see Appendix). Both show again how poetic imaginations can put new and imaginative twists on inherited belief. Both in fact consider the question of the body's demands on our more spiritual inclinations. Donne brings traditional understanding to bear on merely human love, while Marvell comes to a surprisingly balanced view of the dynamic and mutually frustrating relationship between those two "constituent elements." Donne's "Valediction" uses a series of paired opposites to provide its intellectual structure. Marvell, lyric love poet extraordinaire, takes a left turn into a very traditional religious concept—the relationship of the bodily and immediate, to the spiritual and divine. Religious doctrine infuses both poems—the priest's love poem, and the love poet's religious meditation.

We modern readers are perhaps more a sensual than a philosophical lot, more voyeuristic than contemplative, so let's get right to the love poem. But rest assured, Donne will not cater to any prurient interests. Indeed, his speaker is praising the special nature of his and his lady's affection, a bond that *rises above,* and indeed transcends, the physical; it grows almost ethereal. That fact is displayed by many of the remarkable metaphors and similes Donne employs *seriatim* to define it. These remarkable analogies—creative images to which later critics gave the term "metaphysical conceits," or "abstract concepts"—all strive to express the indefinable nature of the affection he and his partner share.

The speaker opens with a two-stanza comparison that establishes a parallel between the nature of their mutual love and the longing of a dying man for heaven. Each item contains that implicit contrast between the pure on the one hand, and the imperfect but all too human on the other:

> As virtuous men pass mildly away,
>　　And whisper to their souls to go,
> Whilst some of their sad friends do say,
>　　"The breath goes now," and some say, "No."
>
> So let us melt, and make no noise,
>　　No tear-floods, nor sigh-tempests move;
> 'Twere profanation of our joys
>　　To tell the laity our love.

There is a lot going on here, but the most intriguing is the analogy Donne draws between the longing of a dying good man for peaceful eternity and the attitude the speaker wants his lover to adopt toward his imminent departure. We never learn where he is going, but we infer it is merely a short journey. He is *not* foretelling his death. Dying is merely analogous, a slightly strained parallel, to departure. Donne introduces here the duality that lies at the poem's intellectual heart—on the one hand, divine and heavenly things; on the other, down-to-earth, bodily and physical matters. While the dying man's spirit is fixed firmly on an eternal reward, the friends around his bed are caught up and fixated on a bodily reality: is he still alive? *He* is having a vision of an apotheosis; *they* are fixated upon his mere breathing out and breathing in. It's a loving and natural concern, but it is, of course, primarily selfish. While he embraces eternity, they lose a dear friend. The two stanzas introduce the first example of that body-spirit dichotomy which the rest of the poem and Marvell's "Dialogue" will further investigate.

Another key declaration here is that the lovers' love is something far superior to that of other mere humans. It's too pure even to mention to "the laity," an ecclesiastical term which suggests in turn that their love is somehow priestly, divine, perhaps even celibate. Even to speak of it would "profane" it. The Latin root of "profane" means "outside the temple." *Their* affection dwells within the sacred precincts.

Donne's third stanza further develops this tension. It contrasts earthquakes to the irregular motions of the starry heavens. Down here, when things shake, damage is caused and we grow fearful. We are much like the men hovering around the dying man in stanza one. *They* press close, arguing over the man's respirations; *we* wonder, wanting to analyze what that horrific earthquake can mean. In contrast to these worldly and physical obsessions, cosmic happenings do no damage in Donne's earth-centered, medieval view of the universe. When a planet, seen from our perspective, seems to back-track in its orbit—that is, seems to trace an "epicycle" in that culture's term—there are no bad results. It's huge, and it's cosmic, but it is in no way harmful.

The next stanza is Donne's most explicit, as he further defines what's wrong with normal human love. It's built too much on the senses, which are the "soul" of such affection; when those bodily elements are apart from each other, their love ceases. Donne uses a clever pun on the word "absence," which in Latin means "away from the senses," to explain why regular humans need each other's physical presence to experience their love. Their bodies constitute their attachment.

That is the sort of love he carefully distinguishes from "ours." For Donne, while the conventional expectation of his day is of a heterosexual love, the nature of the shared affection between the speaker and his lover is gender-less. How can that be? Because theirs is a passion "of the mind." As we will see in the next chapter, William Golding's novel *The Inheritors* rather daringly gives the primitive Neanderthals this purer, more generous sort of love, while "we," the Cro-Magnons—modern man—display attachments that are cruel, violent, self-indulgent, and far from monogamous.

The agony Herbert's speaker undergoes, if taken autobiographically, was Anglican in origin, but it could pass as easily for a rabbi's, an imam's or a Buddhist monk's dark night. The poem captures a universal experience. So, too, with Donne. The relationship being portrayed could be claimed by any combination of lovers and orientations (short, we would hope, of a *ménage*). The bond they share can subsist without "eyes, lips, and hands". It does not rely for its sustenance on holding hands, kissing, or even seeing one another. We may find such a love hard to conceive, but that is precisely Donne's point: their union transcends the corporeal and points to the spiritual. It is a more perfect union, abstracted as it is from the immediate, the tangible, the visible.

That insight leads to some of the poem's most profound images, efforts to use word pictures to capture the ineffable nature of their love. Like St. Paul's vision in "Corinthians" of a Christian's final perfect end, their love shall be changed into something incorruptible (1 Cor 15:52). Paul also notes that "flesh and blood shall not see heaven" (15:50). Just so, Donne's lovers' love rises above flesh and blood and thus approaches the heavenly. The farther they are apart, the purer becomes their union, paradoxically. Their affection grows more absolute the more distant they are. Like gold that gets beaten into "airy thinness," it's as if their love attains a state of almost molecular purity and grows nearly invisible. It ascends from something already golden into something better yet. It is a lovely, a powerful and a profound analysis, achievable only through an imaginative simile. It defies realistic analysis, but we acknowledge its accuracy; paradox often lies at the imaginative heart of a conception of the divine, the transcendent.

The poem concludes with yet another stab at conveying the inexpressible quality of their love. In his heart, the speaker has difficulty thinking of them as two separate entities. But, if forced, he comes up with the "conceit" (concept) of a compass, the kind used for drawing circles. As he travels away from "her" on his anticipated trip, she, the "fixed foot,.../leans and hearkens after" him. The sureness of her love makes his journey like a perfect circle and permits them a final joining upon his return. Like the heavenly spheres in stanza three, his circle is also "just"—perfect—and ends with her, back "where I begun." Their bodies draw together, reflecting their two souls' unity.

◄◦►

Andrew Marvell, whose poetic wit and imagination are as clever as the priestly Donne's, brings to his subject a slightly more tongue-in-cheek attitude. This is perhaps the only indication that the later poet is tackling a traditional theological matter with a lighter, though still quite serious, touch. He still accepts the duality which his era has absorbed from the Christian tradition. This man of the world—Marvell served as a member of Parliament—brings to the issue a more conventional view of the eternal division between body and soul, but his subdued irony does give the body—traditionally the "wrong" member of the pair—the last word.

The soul opens the debate, strong and witty. It laments every particular body part which has it trapped. The bones, the feet, the hands, the senses: all these imprison it. Particularly clever is the idea of its being "manacled by hands." We put handcuffs on prisoners' hands to subdue them; with the manacles removed, the prisoner is freed, but for the soul it is those very hands themselves that trap it, bind it into bodily confinement. Without them, the soul could, like the "virtuous men" Donne pictured in his first stanza, ascend to heaven, leaving earthly accoutrements behind.

Equally clever is the notion that the soul, like Donne's ideal lovers, could do better without the body's eyes. Sure, they give our physical bodies vision, but they "blind" the soul to a clear view of its true and eternal home. The paradox is splendidly profound, repeated by those mortal ears which serve to "deafen" the soul, distracting it from where it wants to go and where it most truly belongs.

The body's lament is just as imaginative. It blames the soul for bringing it alive and making it stand upright. As a result it is in constant danger of falling. It is its "own precipice," a clever, daringly original metaphor. The body realizes that its "frame" is "needless"—a very Christian doctrine, that—and makes the ironic charge that the soul, which Christian doctrine always insists is our lifeline to the heavenly, is no more than an "ill spirit," a force of evil

which has "possessed" the body since birth. For the fore-
seeable future, until its death, the body "can never rest."
It admits that the soul "warms" the body, but makes the
deflating observation that a "fever" could perform that
function just efficiently. Body and soul are mutually unhealthful. Once again, an imaginative Christian writer is
bringing new insights to a millennia-old religious concept.
He repeats the view taught to him by dogma and doctrine,
but he brings to it the more detached cultural biases of
his age, including a more advanced medical appreciation
of those "nerves, arties and veins". It certainly adds both
human and doctrinal insights which the New Testament
gospels never contemplate, at least not so profoundly as
this much later poet.

The soul's second round shows no lessening of dismay;
nor does it lessen the power of the poet's imagination to
evoke it. It continues to explore the paradoxes of its imprisonment. It decries its predicament but analyzes it wit-
tily. True, the soul can feel no sensation, but it can still
feel for the body's recurrent agonies. Hence the paradox:
"I feel, that cannot feel, the pain." The first use is, shall
we say, in the Clintonian sense; the second, in the strictly
sensory. The soul finds itself forced to undergo not only
recurring illnesses, but "what's worse, the cure." Longing
for heaven, "the port," it is continually "shipwrecked into
health" whenever the body locates an effective doctor!
Marvell shows us that one of the great pleasures in our
lives, recovering from a painful or scary disease, is for the
soul a matter of spiritual desolation.

It is the body, however, that gets the poet's final word,
perhaps reflecting an era and culture more attuned to the
here and now and less fixated on the eternal than, say,
Chaucer's. The body in its final say condemns the soul for
exposing it to those emotions that are unique to the soul
but that cause the body its own set of recurring agonies.

Hope and fear; love and hatred; joy and sorrow—these are emotions of the spirit; still, they intrude into the body's sphere of perceptions. They create unpleasant sensations. And those emotions are further worsened by two forces we humans normally revere: memory and knowledge. Their only effect on the body is to prolong its experience of that wide range of emotions, over which it exercises no control. Bad enough to experience them in the first place; memory makes us replay them over and over.

The final simile Marvell puts into the body's mouth is a powerful one. It charges that it is the soul that forces the body to sin. The soul, says the body, is like an architect— possibly one who regularly employs Donne's "twin, stiff compasses" to create a blueprint—who takes those natural "green trees" from the forest and shapes them ("hews" them) for other purposes, alien to their true nature. It is as if the soul is the scientist or engineer, chopping down or uprooting the natural body and then trying to craft it in unnatural ways. This reflection plays a nice, perhaps even devastating, variation on the traditional Christian doctrine that holds the body guilty of drawing us down to our worst instincts—lust, anger, and the five other deadly sins. Here, Marvell suggests it is the thinking and emotional soul who possesses those drives and makes the poor body the means whereby they are experienced in our life. Notice, too, that not only does the body speak last but also it has fourteen lines, not the ten previously allotted to each side in this debate.

Donne employed traditional Christian doctrine in clever and imaginative ways to a love relationship. Marvell's poetic vision is a comparably clever, witty and original take on traditional Christian teaching. It forces the faithful of his era to stop and adopt a new perspective on "what we've always been taught," thus fulfilling the creative artist's central obligation: to bring traditional belief under an imaginative microscope and thereby force his readers to reexamine those inherited truths.

Works Cited

Donne, John. "A Valediction Forbidding Mourning." P. 891 in *Norton Anthology of Literature*. Vol. 1. New York: Norton, 1968.

Marvell, Andrew. "A Dialogue Between Soul and Body." P. 985 in *Norton Anthology of Literature*. Vol.1. New York: Norton, 1968.

A Geological Interlude

Tennyson's In Memoriam
& the Rise of Science

There rolls the deep where grew the tree.
O earth, what changes hast thou seen!
There where the long street roars, hath been
The stillness of the central sea.
　　　　—Alfred, Lord Tennyson, Poem CXXII, 1–4

In 1849, Alfred, Lord Tennyson, published a massive poem called *In Memoriam*, consisting of more than 130 poems, each several stanzas in length. The lines above number only four, but they are crucial for the investigation we are about to undertake in chapter 5—a comparison between the work of a deeply pious seventeenth-century Christian poet, John Milton, and that of a twentieth-century novelist and skeptic, William Golding. They reveal some drastically changed insights into, and assumptions about, the physical earth, its history, and its successive inhabitants. Such changes reflect the astonishing discoveries made by science in the three centuries that lapsed between Milton and Golding. The effect of those scientific investigations on the prior ages' dogmatic certitudes is incalculable; it deserves at least some brief attention in this study of the evolving literary responses to established dogma and proclaimed doctrine.

Though Tennyson is not a writer we are singling out for detailed artistic analysis, we can note in passing the poetic craftsmanship he puts to work in this brief passage. As he paints the notion of vast geological change that is his focus, the second line announces the concept; the others offer two vivid examples. He dramatizes the change by contrasting the single syllables and long vowels of "long street roars" with the four "s" sounds in the final line. Those sounds picture the soft quiet of the ocean depths that once ruled the busy urban scene (the heart of London perhaps) which he now observes and whose loud "roar" he hears.

The very idea of time's vast extent, and of the slow and enormous changes on earth which it has witnessed, is a million miles, metaphorically—and more than a billion years, literally—from Milton's seventeenth-century idea of the earth's recent creation. Milton's picture of the heavens in *Paradise Lost* is heavily indebted to the pre-Copernican vision of the universe with the earth at its center, the same one Donne pictured in his "Valediction." Even after the recognition of our heliocentric local cosmos took hold, another century and a half was required after Milton before scientific investigations—many of them carried out, in England anyway, by curious but determined amateurs—began to make an impact on Europeans' long-held view of the earth itself. In Charles Gillispie's remarkable survey of this era, *Genesis and Geology,* we learn that, at its start, many scientists still used "their talents to [express] the majesty and wonder of God's revelation to mankind, a message which could be read not only in the inspired writings but also in His book of Nature" (4). Science basically hewed to the notion expressed by eighteenth-century writer Colin McLarin that "the least examination of Nature will show plain footsteps of Divine Creation" (quoted in Gillispie, 12). Even the supreme scientist of the era, Newton, did not quarrel with that fundamental given.

In contrast, the eminent nineteenth-century scientist Thomas Henry Huxley shrewdly observed that "extinguished theologians lie about the cradle of every science as the strangled snakes beside that of Hercules" (quoted in Gillispie, 1). Science began to make observations toward the end of the eighteenth century the implications of which could no longer be ignored. In 1795, crucially, James Hutton's seminal geological work, *Theory of the Earth,* began the slow process whereby traditional confidence in Biblical accounts of the earth's formation would be shaken. Serious doubts, particularly about nature, timing and effects of the Flood, were growing; Hutton's geological studies raised arresting questions about the age of the earth. He cast into doubt, according to Stephen Baxter in his *Ages in Chaos,* the date of creation which Bishop James Ussher had proclaimed in the 1650s. He confidently assured believers that it occurred on the autumn solstice, in 4004 BC, "four thousand years before the birth of Christ Himself" (21). That date "became imprinted in the mass consciousness for two centuries or more" (17). To question Ussher was, many felt, to attack religion, even though his effort to determine that instant of creation was itself a self-evident exercise in imaginative invention and arithmetical deduction. As Baxter notes, "Hutton replaced the hand of God with the great pressure of time, long aeons of it. And deep geological time is Hutton's wonderful and terrible legacy, to us and to every generation to come" (4). He goes on to point out the huge influence of the Scottish philosopher David Hume on the geologist's thinking:

> In the end, said Hume, all knowledge originates in experience; everything else you have to infer. And that was how Hutton had come to think about geology...[which] deals with the interior of the Earth, the depths of the sea—even the deep past and far future— all places we cannot observe...[So] we have to begin with experience...We can look only at rocks in the present...and we can observe only the processes acting on them. (131)

Hutton, working on Hume's philosophical principles, brings the true scientific method to bear on what had been considered sacrosanct—God's watery and rocky handiwork.

The effect was revolutionary. As Gillispie notes, "Certain consequences of Hutton's views became immediately apparent. Most obvious was the vastness of geological time which his theory demanded." After all, "No observed change had taken place in all of recorded history. Throughout how many inconceivable ages, then, must this endless rising and falling of continents have been proceeding" (48)? Indeed, a follower of Hutton, John Playfair, provides a fine dramatic and literary account of the moment that he and Hutton came across an outcropping of rock on Arran Island, a magical geological locale that finally confirmed the latter's hypothesis about the earth's slow and gradual formation. As Baxter puts it, quite dramatically, "This small Scottish island was to serve as the scale model for a planet" (157). He begins to retell the moment: "When they landed they could see clearly how...the older strata had been tilted on end and eroded before younger sediments...had been laid flat on top" (159–60). Playfair himself continues the story: "What clearer evidence could we have of the different formation of these rocks, and of the long interval which separated their formation, had we actually seen them emerging from the bosom of the deep?" (qtd. in Baxter, 160). Those last few words very nearly evoke the world of endless, slow and vast change that Tennyson would draw not long after.

It is hard to over-estimate the effect of such a revolution in Europe's *weltanschauung*, the commonly-accepted framework of ideas by which people conceive the world they inhabit. Tennyson reflected the revolution geology had wrought, and it was but the first such shock. Ten years later, in 1859, Darwin would publish his *On the Origin of*

Species, a book that went beyond rocks and contemplated life itself; it would drive another nail into the coffin of fundamentalist belief, though even today, sad to report, diehards remain. We still await that ultimate nail.

Works Cited

Baxter, Stephen. *Ages in Chaos: James Hutton and the Discovery of Deep Time.* New York: Forge, 2006.

Gillispie, Charles Coulson. *Genesis and Geology: The Impact of Scientific Discoveries Upon Religious Beliefs in the Decades before Darwin.* New York: Harper, 1959.

5

William Golding & John Milton

Twin Falls

The two authors to be discussed in this chapter make a perfect pairing for our purposes. One is a superb specimen of a man of devout faith, dedicated to the creation of a self-proclaimed literary task of deep piety: "to justify the ways of God to man" (Milton, *Paradise Lost,* I. 26). He was a fervent Protestant and so his take on religious matters may be said to be informed by the same sort of fervor the first Christians might have felt. Say what you will about Puritan evangelism, it was in any event a recapturing of the church's early intensity, with an extra Puritan dollop of institutional hostility. Milton is perhaps the consummate, literate Protestant, daring to do as a lone but devout poetic creator what for a millennia and a half had been the province of a single but vast ecclesiastical authority. Thus, he is in a way the ideal creative artist for our purposes, the supreme exemplar of a writer burrowing into a sacred text and emerging with a self-contained and brilliant recreation of that Scripture. By doing so, he created a literary work that has all the force and authority of divine revelation. What Dickens would do for Christmas, Milton achieved for The Fall.

William Golding, on the other hand, in his 1955 novel *The Inheritors,* writes from a twentieth-century perspective; he brings to his analysis the sort of detachment encouraged by several centuries of science and the disinterest which the scientific method demands. No doubt there are paleoanthropologists who will quarrel with the novelist's fictional creation, just as many theologians may find fault with Milton's vision of heaven, hell, and earth. In any event, just as Hutton's daring but thorough, objective and wholly responsible observations form the intellectual basis for Tennyson's poetic lines, so, too, does Darwin's hypothesis of evolving species inspire Golding's fictional task. As Baxter notes,

> For better or worse, Darwin transformed our view of our place in the universe. Humans too are not the outcome of a divine design, but simply the products of the relentless workings of natural laws, just like rivers and mountains, beetles and whales. (208)

William Golding's The Inheritors

Golding's novel is characteristically imaginative and daringly original. It has a small and narrow focus, both in terms of elapsed time (three or four days) and arena of action (roughly a square mile). In simplest terms, it narrates the tale of what Golding portrays as the last small tribe of Neanderthal humans; they encounter and are, one by one, killed off by an early tribe of "us"—Cro-Magnons. Golding makes these two species' encounter iconic—the end of one era and the arrival of another. As you might expect from the author of *Lord of the Flies*, "we" do not come out very admirably. Like the young Ralph in that famous novel, the Neanderthals are peaceful and considerate. The new humans are more like Jack—violent, cruel, intolerant, carnivorous, and sexually aggressive.

"The people" is the term these barely articulate Neanderthals use about themselves; "the new people" is the term they apply to the invaders. The Neanderthals are remarkably sweet, docile and, for the most part, trusting. They may find the newcomers strange-smelling, but they bear them no ill-will; they trust them implicitly. They feel kindly toward them, in the word's original, communal sense seen previously in *Macbeth.* "We," however, find the Neanderthal inhabitants horrific. Golding opens the book quoting a remark by H. G. Wells that "some dim racial remembrance" of these folks' "shambling gait, hairy bodies, strong teeth may be the germ of the ogre in folklore." In *Lord of the Flies,* Golding took a comforting Victorian tale of survival and ingenuity and made it into an allegory of human evil. *The Inheritors* employs a similar inversion: it makes the monsters the good guys and, while the Cro-Magnons are undeniably resourceful, they are, in a key evolutionary notion, rootless.

Perhaps that is the inevitable price evolution has paid for the possibility of "progress." The new people are destined to displace the Neanderthals, who represent a very static and very unimaginative, if reliable, lifestyle. Their existence, and that of their many generations of forebears, is built around two homes—a cave by the sea in winter, then a return to a protected platform in spring for the other half of the year. They have no comprehension of, and thus no interest in, the very concept of progress, of movement, of doing new things. As they return to their platform, Lok says, "The stone is a good stone. It has not gone away" (31). Fa confirms, "Today is like yesterday is like tomorrow" (46). Primitive and unswerving conservatism defines their value system and world view.

In what proves to be a fascinating doctrinal touch, Golding sets his tale near a large and loud waterfall. Its roar is near the platform next to the swift stream, which feeds that loud fall. Since they fear water, the tribe fondly assumes it is safe from any foes. The new people, on the other hand, seem to have traveled across the sea and, in the course of the story, portage themselves, their canoes, and their belongings up the river, past the falls, and onto the mountain-ringed lake which feeds that fall. The new people's murderous and fearful elimination of the placid

Neanderthals thus takes place entirely near the waterfall. By the end of the tragedy, it also thereby marks the place where modern man arises.

Golding thus makes that physical feature, the novel's key setting, into a statement both sociological and theological: it is the true site of "the fall." There is no apple and Garden of Eden, and there is no single act of disobedience. Rather, our actions at Golding's waterfall demonstrate what we *homo sapiens* are; it is what evolution has made us. Golding suggests further that, as the title suggests, it is our species' memory of the fall from which we moderns inherited the mastery of the planet that affected in turn the theological conception of the biblical "fall."

To get a fuller sense of Golding's profoundly moral and deeply pessimistic insight, it helps to examine his Neanderthals in some detail. Not only loving and deeply communal, they exchange ideas through a limited vocabulary and also, perhaps as primitive compensation, something resembling telepathy. Perhaps most significant, and here Golding was far ahead of his time politically, the tribe is matriarchal. As they put it, thinking as usual in firm pigeonholes, "The woman is for Oa, the man for the pictures in his head" (70). The women of the tribe are in touch with the earth goddess and speak with her ultimate authority; men bring recollections of earlier experiences to the table and thus represent practical wisdom. It is Oa who defines the tribe's key principles of life: fertility, kindness and community.

They are, in short, a primitive effort at *Macbeth*'s Christian model of a loving commonwealth; they are a much kinder form of Abner Snopes's patriarchal and truly primitive tribal unit we will encounter in Faulkner's "Barn Burning." The group consists of three apparently monogamous couples. In addition to Fa and Lok (and their daughter Liku) there are Ha and Nil, who have a "new one" just born. There are also an old man and an old woman. They are essentially vegetarians, though to us their diet is most unappealing; tree fungi, or "ears" as they call them, are its staple.

Golding makes the case for female superiority, a sensible corollary to the tribe's reverence for female divinity. The most persuasive occurs early in the novel when he shows Fa, clearly the brightest and bravest member of the tribe, having a brilliant idea. She has always, mindlessly, accepted the tribe's habit of living on the platform but on this day, as they trail out to fetch "pale grubs and awakened shoots" and then carry their finds back to the platform, she has an inspiration:

> Fa frowned and munched.
> "If the patch were nearer..."
> She swallowed her mouthful with a gulp.
> "I have a picture. The good food is growing. Not here. It is growing by the fall."
> Lok laughed at her.
> "No plant like this grows near the fall."
> ...She tried again.
> "But if—see this picture." (49)

Golding is showing Fa trying to conceive of and convey the idea of agriculture—of moving their food source nearer their living quarters—but Lok just doesn't get it. The tribe as a whole lacks the imagination to act upon the insights of their brightest member. The stuck-in-a-rut others merely laugh. Conservatism has its dangers. Fatal ones, as it proves.

The tribe's inevitably incomplete vision of the new people still offers a devastating indictment of our ways. The tribe's perceptions are almost uniformly negative, and Fa's most devastating comment is that "Oa did not bring them out of her belly" (173). In their language and theology, she is calling us god-forsaken. The newcomers are regularly compared to dark pale things, beetles in dead tree bark, and so on. The Neanderthals' first awareness of these intruders is their strange smell; but the second is the way they build fires, coils of useless smoke (51). Those coils introduce a key image for the theology Golding is invoking.

In fact, some of his most imaginative touches involve the way he has adapted Judeo-Christian motifs from the Garden of Eden story, over and above "the fall." When Lok, a likeable but mentally weak man and the only male survivor of the new people's homicidal intrusions, catches a glimpse of Ha's killer, he follows him to the stream above the falls. The new creature is described vividly twice. The first time Lok sees him as part of a rock in the stream. "As he watched him, one of the farther rocks began to change shape. At one side a small bump appeared and the top of the rock swelled, the hump fined off at its base and elongated again, then halved its height" (79). Golding is working quite subtly with a distinct image, whose character he'll soon reveal. Next, Lok observes the base of a lone birch tree which seems "unduly thick...impossibly thick." And then: "The blob of darkness seemed to coagulate around the stem like a drop of blood on a stick. It lengthened, thickened again, lengthened" (79). By now the image is both vivid and unmistakable. The new man moves like a snake. Those undisciplined coils of smoke which their fires emit were an early hint at the image; now we see that these very people are indeed profoundly snake-like. It's an imaginative and devastating adaptation of the story in Genesis. Golding then reinforces the moment of the encounter by reintroducing the fall. When Lok tries to call out to that black blob human, "either the creature was deaf or the ponderous fall erased the words" (80). The fall prevents communication between us and our more primitive predecessors. Think of the implications. Here, there is no Eve. And no tempter. *We* are the serpent. Or, as Walt Kelly once had his comic strip character Pogo say, "We have met the enemy and he is us."

Another piercing transformation of the sacred original occurs when Lok and Fa stealthily climb a tree to observe the midnight revels of the new ones. They view the scene closely, observing but unobserved, from deep within the branches of a tree. Golding gives that tree extra resonance. He says it "grew so huge he might think the clouds were really caught in its branches" (100), a metaphor which lends it almost mythic proportions. It is also that leafy enclosure that serves to educate them, for it is there that these last two Neanderthals receive the fullest, prolonged taste of what we modern humans are like. They see that it is our DNA and the drunken, sexually aggressive culture it leads us to create that constitute the evil in the world—not a single act of disobedience. The tree from which they observe these things is, in short, their tree of knowledge. It follows further that there is no paradise to which to return; we murdered its last occupants.

There is an even more powerful parallel, one that reflects great literary sophistication on Golding's part. At the end of the novel, the omniscient narrative viewpoint assumes full control. We watch the creature Lok, whose mind and perceptions we have gotten to know intimately in the book's first twelve chapters, curl into a fetal position around the ashes of the dying tribe's dead fire. He expires. As if to confirm that this is indeed the end of an evolutionary era, the ice goddesses whom he and Fa had earlier visited choose that moment to collapse. We modern and confidently scientific sorts know what these "goddesses" really "are": crevices of mountain ice, frozen into the cliff face by the winter's cold. With the coming of spring warmth, they gradually melt, loosen, and finally crash into the lake below. Our view of nature as "red in tooth and claw" is another phrase from Tennyson's *In Memoriam* that has become part of our vocabulary about, and our vision of, nature. Tennyson's harsh conception instructs us that violence wins out, that a stronger or shrewder tribe or species will come along. Clearly, to us moderns, these Neanderthal folks are doomed to extinction. Golding, however, is up to something far more mythical and more literary.

Golding's depiction of nature gives him yet another chance to equate women with brains and imagination, a compliment in keeping with the matriarchal nature of their tribal order and the assignment of religious authority to women. It is appropriate, therefore, that the tribe see, in those ice goddesses to whom they return every spring, a projection and emanation of Oa, a reminder of her lasting authority. When the omniscient point of view shows Lok curling up to die, there follows an account of the crumbling of the ice figures. It is a significant and deeply allusive moment.

> The ice crowns of the mountain were a-glitter. They
> welcomed the sun. There was a sudden tremendous
> noise that...engulfed the water noises, rolled along
> the mountains, boomed from cliff to cliff and spread
> in a tangle of vibrations over the sunny forests and out
> towards the sea. (222)

The loud and reverberant crashes mark the coming of spring; but at this moment they symbolize even more. They convey the death of the old order. They confirm the fall.

In doing so Golding makes another subtle allusion to Tennyson's long work, which, though not much read by Americans, would be more than familiar to Golding's fellow British readers. Tennyson names something he calls "spires of ice" and mentions them in the context of similar revolutionary changes the poet was observing in the political world of the 1840s. "Ill for him who wears a crown" is his warning of impending doom for traditional monarchies, followed by the key image: "they tremble, the sustaining crags/The spires of ice they topple down/And molten up and roar in flood" (CXVII, lines 11–12). I would suggest that the visual resemblance of Tennyson's image to the novel's graphic scene is no coincidence. Golding alludes to Tennyson's vision to confirm that what the novel has pictured is the end of an era. Tennyson sees it more hopefully; for Golding, however, it confirms the tragic emergence of a cruel but determined species.

Both Golding's novel and Tennyson's long poem evoke a sense of earth's and life's vast transformations. The irony is that, while Tennyson was looking toward the rise of democracy and tyranny's decline, Golding is far more pessimistic. In his tale of the fall that gave rise to modern humans, Golding paints us as rapacious, sexually indulgent, violent, homicidal—all this in spite of our admittedly superior consciousness, advanced technology, and forward-moving determination. The novel ends with one *homo sapiens* gazing out to the receding horizon: "he could not see if the line of darkness had an ending" (223). The imagery evokes Conrad's equally pessimistic novella *Heart of Darkness*. The events surrounding the fall hardly foretell any human improvement, other than an almost genetic drive toward seeking out new territory.

Conveniently for our purposes here, Golding is also echoing Milton. His description of those crashing "ice goddesses" recalls an image in Book IX of *Paradise Lost* with Satan's offer of the apple to Eve. When she yields to Satan's guile,

> ...she pluck'd, she ate:
> Earth felt the wound, and Nature from her seat
> Sighing through all her works gave sign of woe
> That all was lost. (IX.781–84)

The sighing of all of nature here is an obvious parallel to Golding's more vivid and much louder climax. Clearly well-read, the British author alludes to two works simultaneously, Milton's and Tennyson's. Three, if you include the ultimate progenitor, Genesis. It is a further reminder of the continuing, indeed accretive role of literature in furthering the process of doctrinal interpretation and adjustment.

John Milton's *Paradise Lost*

John Milton's *Paradise Lost* is a remarkable masterpiece of Christian literature. The English critic Dr. Samuel Johnson said that its sacred subject made it superior even to Virgil and Homer. The Puritan poet embarked in 1667 on a daringly vast scheme—to take the few lines from Genesis and transform them into his twelve book epic, *Paradise Lost*. It covers Lucifer's war in Heaven with God and his banishment from heaven, the founding of Hell, the creation of the earth, and man's fall and subsequent expulsion from paradise. It is over 10,000 lines long (Johnson admitted "no one has wished it longer") and it has been the subject of lengthy volumes of analysis and criticism. For our more modest purposes, we will focus on Book IX, in which Milton dramatizes the actual fall. While it is a work of deep piety and reverence, it is also the work of a brilliant and thoughtful poet. It therefore attempts not only to do justice to its two eventually fallen heroes, Adam and Eve, but also to give a powerful, indeed unforgettable portrait of Satan, the former angel Lucifer. It is a profoundly satisfying work of both high drama and incisive psychology.

Milton was a deeply religious man who was committed to the Puritan cause against King Charles I, a rebellion which led to that monarch's execution by Oliver Cromwell's forces in 1649. Milton narrowly avoided prison following the 1660 Restoration of the executed monarch's son, Charles II. Like many zealous believers, Milton has something of that same evangelical spirit we assume drove the early fathers of the church. His spirit and intellectual capacity were fortunately far more open to, and welcoming of, the implications of holy writ than those of his fundamentalist brethren and sisters of today. Nor, consistent with their commitment to infallible divine inspiration, would they ever consider Milton's work as comparably inspired. Many less doctrinaire readers would disagree. I certainly do. As both a literary critic and a modern thinker engaged with biblically-inspired writing, I consider it perfectly within my province to observe, appraise and, where proper, admire the "take" this deeply religious man and esteemed poet brings to those very few words from Genesis, which were in truth the genesis of his vast epic.

The parallel with Golding is also a contrast. The novelist uses the arriving Cro-Magnon *homo sapiens* tribe as representative of us modern men and women; the Neanderthals serve as the admirable but sadly ineffective version of prelapsarian man. "Lapsarian" comes from the Latin term *lapsus* for "fall"—the "prelapsarian" man is, thus, man "before the fall." Both writers are exploring the nature of humankind, its character and behavior, before the fall. Milton has it easier, with doctrinal backing. Satan seeks out "the only two of mankind, but in them/ The whole included Race" (415–16). He means them to stand for us, both as we were in paradise and, after the temptation, as we are yet today. In Genesis, there is scant dialogue and indeed the entire temptation and fall lasts a mere six verses (3:1 through 3:6).

Milton is especially fine in the dialogue he creates between our first father and mother, much of it with convincing psychological insights. An especially effective touch occurs early in the book, when we meet the First Couple preparing for the day. He makes a touching equation when Adam makes a pious observation about God's demands: Yes, He urges labor, but He also allows time for "refreshment." It can be of either "food or talk," the latter of which Milton calls "Food of the mind." It can also take the form of "this sweet intercourse/Of looks and smiles, for smiles from Reason flow/To brute denied, and are of love the food" (238–40). Milton paints the sort of paradise that would appeal, first, to a thoughtful academic like himself but also to a man who harbors a natural fondness for conjugal bliss. Love, he insists, is built on thoughtful discourse and smiling exchanges, all of them prompted by Reason. We naturally applaud Milton's insistence on the force Reason played in us before we fell. John Donne, you will recall, terms it "God's Viceroy in us," reminding us of its continuing divine availability, though our sinful urges often disable its effectiveness.

Some of Milton's other definitions of the ideal, however—especially his view of the proper marital relations of man and woman, and of woman's proper role—may well prove less appealing to our modern, enlightened, egalitarian tastes. To his vision we must bring some patient tolerance. Milton, after all, is speaking for his generation and is indeed a spokesman for traditional religious views that are still held in some quarters even today, and not just by Christians. We learn, for one thing, that the angel Gabriel has warned only Adam about Satan's imminent approach. Eve, because she is considered either less trustworthy or intellectually less competent, must learn of it only by overhearing their conversation. That male angel-to-angelic-man chat suggests a divinely-sanctioned preference for guys. Later, as they greet each other in the Garden on their final day of bliss, Adam thanks Eve for her willingness to tend the garden and praises her, "for nothing lovelier can be found/In woman, than to study household good,/And good works in her husband to promote" (232–34). What we today call feminist thought did not arise for another century and a half after Milton, perhaps as a by-product of the Enlightenment. It seems it takes eons for a confident reliance on Reason and fair play to displace society's acquired appeal to divine sanction for men's superiority.

Adam's words here echo the rhetorical appeals Eve and Adam have exchanged earlier in the day. Adam shows concern for Eve, not for her strength to resist but for the shame the effort might cost her.

> For hee who attempts, though in vain, at least asperses
> The tempted with dishonor foul, suppos'd
> Not corruptible of Faith, nor proof
> Against temptation. (296–99)

It's an insult to her reputed virtue even to contemplate her yielding, and it is also a clever appeal to her pride. But upon inspection it seems flimsy. To whom would she have to defend her honor? Adam is her sole audience and judge. Aside from God and the various angels, it's a small human world!

Nonetheless, her answer is deeply moral: "What is Faith, Love, Virtue unassay'd/Alone, without exterior help sustained?" (335–36). Milton has Eve make two points here. On the one hand, we can hardly trust to our inner moral strength if it is never tested. This echoes his position in his famous essay on freedom of the press, "Areopagitica," in which he also argues against virtue that remains "cloistered"; he insists it is far better to prove itself by "salleying out to meet the adversary." Secondly, Eve rightly observes that it is not much of a paradise if we have to withstand the threat by ourselves, on our own. "Frail is our happiness if this be so,/And *Eden* were no *Eden* thus expos'd" (340–41).

Adam ends their debate with another rather patriarchal rebuke, insisting that "Trial will come unsought./ Would'st thou approve [prove] thy constancy, approve/ First thy obedience" (367–68). He's saying that silent obedience is a follower's surest way to demonstrate her loyalty. But Adam does not insist, a choice for which she, unfairly but all too humanly, will later upbraid him, when it is too late, saying in effect, "Why didn't you stop me?" Adam adds the loving reassurance that she should "Go; for thy stay, not free, absents thee more" (372). He makes the incisive psychological point that he feels more removed from her in spirit if she remains with him unwillingly. Free will and free departure lie at the heart of their ideal harmony. She assures him that she is safe because a devil as proud as Satan would not dare to approach the weaker vessel and fail. "The willinger I go nor much expect/A foe so proud will first the weaker seek" (382–83).

Adam's patriarchal view has not changed at the Book's end. Indeed, Adam blames her for their great error, and draws the following lesson, echoes of which still reverberate today: "Thus it shall befall/Him who to worth in women overtrusting/Lets her will rule: restraint she will not brook" (1182–85). Milton has Adam voice a lasting warning about giving women too much authority, including a clever pun: "befall" foreshadows "the fall". While a reliance on critical thought should teach us not to judge another era's and culture's ideals, this last prohibition does strike us moderns as ethically wrong. It's also, as many of us have learned on the job, not a recommended stance upon which to build a marriage.

◄○►

Eclipsing the psychological interactions between Adam and Eve is Milton's incomparable portrait of Satan. The only real Biblical reference is to a serpent in Genesis 3:6; even there, Satan is not named. From that almost non-existent hint, Milton spins out a masterful narrative of evil, a narrative that springs both from his own imagination and from his sharp observation of political intrigue and behavior. The result is a probing psychological portrait, one that has to have been inspired by Shakespeare, a dramatist Milton admired. The depths of character which that predecessor discovered and presented in such characters as Brutus (in *Julius Caesar*), Hotspur (in *Henry IV, Part One*), and above all Hamlet were models crying out for imitation. And as a model for evil, of course, the devilish Iago from *Othello* was superb. As a further tribute, Milton also adopted the playwright's unrhymed iambic pentameter—blank verse. The profundity and extent of Milton's portrait is one that is appropriate for the bringer of "all that woe" (I. 3)—our fall—and appropriate indeed for the complex nature of a fallen angel—a creature of deep feelings, driving ambition, and sharp intellect. Milton devotes huge swaths of the epic to him; Book IX offers particularly poignant and sustained glimpses into his mind, his heart and his subtle machinations.

Before the fallen angel even commences his evil machinations, Satan's first challenge is logistical, his solution shrewd. He has the full range of animals in whom to conceal himself, but "found/The serpent subtlest Beast of all the field." After prolonged meditation, he chooses him

> Fit vessel, fittest Imp of fraud, in whom
> To enter, and his dark suggestions hide
> From sharpest sight: for in the wily Snake
> Whatever sleights none would suspicious mark. (89–92)

At his first sight of the earth, Satan, though still consumed with jealousy and wounded pride from his expulsion from heaven, cannot help adoring it. His soliloquy is Shakespearean in rhythm and imagery. He voices Milton's subtle theological comment that our world is a "seat worthier of the gods, as built/With second thoughts, reforming what was old" (100–101). That's an insight that one will not find in the first book of the Pentateuch; it suggests God has erred and tried to improve on a second try. It is, like much of Milton's evocation of Satan and of his seduction of Adam and Eve, a personal and poetic re-telling and original creation of ideas barely whispered in Holy Writ.

He praises not only earth's looks and but its location, voicing perhaps the last vestiges of the old, pre-Copernican vision of the universe with the earth at its center.

> ...As God in Heav'n
> Is Center, yet extends to all, so thou
> Centr'ing receiv'st from all those Orbs: in thee,
> Nor in themselves, all their known virtue appears.
> (107–10)

With typical satanic narcissism—that is perhaps the besetting sin bequeathed to us by the fall, after our innocent and selfless life in the Garden—his next thought turns to himself. "With what delight could I have walkt thee round/ If I could joy in ought" (114–15). It is brought home to him powerfully how much he has lost by being driven out of heaven and excluded from earth, this second heaven. His despair is poignant and, since we humans share in the world he caused to fall, we feel his pain and grief:

> ...but I in none of these
> Can find place or refuge; and the more I see
> Pleasures around me, so much more I feel
> Torment within me. (118–21)

Milton paints Satan's alienation as being like the same estrangement felt and voiced by Golding's Cro-Magnons.

Knowing he has no escape from this agony, his only recompense is to make others as poorly off as he; he has

> No hope to make myself less miserable
> By what I seek, but others to make such as I...
> For only in destroying I find ease
> To my relentless thoughts. (126–30)

And that sense of accomplishment has a further psychological benefit. It will make him more admired by his fellow infernal powers, noting that he will have "in one day...marr'd/What he, *Almighty* styled, six Nights and Days/Continu'd making" (136–38). Satan not only questions God's right to that omnipotent adjective, but vaunts himself as six times more powerful if he can destroy God's new creation.

Milton has his villain repeat his combination of despair and admiration as the climactic encounter approaches. We watch Milton the epic dramatist building suspense; the action moves toward its ultimate tragic collision. Eve he establishes as a creature of both visual and aromatic beauty. Once again, Milton takes a picture only implicit in Genesis—"the rib...he made into a woman and brought her to him"—and derives from it an invention almost wholly of poetic imagining, an enormously impressive act of original poetic creation. It far outshines God's own creative act as sketched in by the Old Testament's fictional creators.

> ...Eve separate he spies
> Veil'd in a cloud of Fragrance, where she stood,
> Half spi'd, so thick the roses bushing round
> About her glow'd.... (424–27)

To the suspense Milton adds pity when he, the reporter of the moment, grieves that while she is intent on propping up all the flowers in her care, she herself is "from her prop so farr, and storm so nigh."

But at this instant comes another poignant reminder that angelic and appreciative parts of Satan remain, even after his rebellion and banishment. Here, as throughout, we feel for him. That, after all, is only natural: Satan *is* what he has made us. He stands amazed at Eve's beauty: "Such pleasure took the serpent to behold/This Flow'ry Plat, the sweet recess of Eve, thus early, thus alone" (455–57). He cannot stir, because

> Her graceful Innocence, her every Aire
> Of gesture or least action overaw'd
> His malice, and with rapine sweet bereav'd
> His fierceness of the fierce intent it brought. (459–62)

The effect is powerful and profound.

> That space the Evil one abstracted stood
> From his own evil, and for the time remain'd
> Stupidly good, of enmity disarm'd,
> Of guile, of hate, of envy, of revenge. (463–66)

The moment affirms that there is (was) such goodness in the world before the fall that even a person of mighty power and evil intent could be "pulled out" himself by meeting it face to face. Milton, a Latin scholar, well knew the original meaning of the verb "abstracted". One of my favorite examples of such bi-lingual word-use occurs when Satan first arrives outside of Eden. He finds an entry via a river: "And with it rose Satan/Involv'd with mist" (74–75). In addition to the normal English sense of involvement is the Latin concept of "rotating" or "wheeling" within the cloud. It's an early hint of those spiraling mazes with which he will move toward and then with Eve.

Satan is not released for long. His envy reignites, for

> That hot Hell that always in him burns,
> Though in mid-heav'n, soon ended his delight
> And tortures him more now, the more he sees
> Of pleasures not for him ordain'd. (467–70)

Milton the poetic linguist then plays with the two meanings of "recollect"—"remember" as well as "gather together again." "Then soon/Fierce hate he recollects, and all his thoughts of mischief, gratulating, thus excites." He dances his coils before her and approaches,

> ...not with indented wave,
> Prone on the ground, as since, but on his reare
> Circular base of rising folds, that [towered]
> Fold above fold a surging Maze, his Head
> Crested aloft, and Carbuncle his eyes. (497–500)

It's not just a powerful visual image, Virgilian in intensity; the idea of the maze nicely predicts the endless complications of evil he brings with him into our world and our moral life.

Milton is incisive in developing the sorts of psychological appeals that a devilish mind might invent to appeal to our first mother. Adam, alas, was correct: Satan, a proud patriarch, knows the woman is the weaker vessel and is relieved to find her alone and vulnerable. And he brings to the contest a large armory of wily arguments and seductive behaviors. First, he

> Curled many a tortuous wreath in sight of Eve,
> To lure her eye…: Oft he bowed
> His turret crest, and sleek enamel'd neck,
> Fawning and lick'd the ground on which she trod.
> (517–26)

Her attention gained, he intrigues her by his description of a marvelous plant that, he claims, has given him the power of speech; he convinces her to follow him. Earlier he moved his maze of coils. Now "Hee leading swiftly roll'd/ In tangles, and made intricate seem straight,/To mischief swift" (631–33). His manner of moving is a metaphor for his evil intent and its ease of achievement. Isaiah foretold that the messiah will make "the crooked straight;" that is the exact reverse of Satan's devilish strategy here. Handel, in the aria "Every valley shall be exalted" from his *Messiah,* paints Isaiah's promised fulfillment musically, "crooked" on five alternating notes, "straight" on one.

We need not walk through the entire seduction, but some points should be noticed, reminders of the brilliant poetry and psychology this creative artist could generate from that profound but concise biblical text. One is the simile Milton comes up with to describe Satan as he commences his sale. Milton has him make "a shew of Zeale and Love/To Man and indignation at his wrong" and then, like an actor: "New part puts on, and as to passion mov'd/Fluctuates disturb'd" (665–68). The Puritans tried to ban acting in Shakespeare's day, and succeeded in having it moved to what were then considered the evil suburbs. The Puritans of Milton's time had been overthrown by the Restoration, but the poet retains his distrust of playacting. He implies that those who practice it are in effect the spawn of Satan.

When he leads her to the plant, Satan proceeds to reverently address this mere creation, a key reminder that to eat of the fruit is to turn away from the Creator. When Eve sees which tree it is, her first obedient response is to quote God's command: human reason is sovereign in all other matters, but regarding the tree, He draws the line. The flaws in God's logic give Satan the perfect opportunity for a persuasive speech, praising the tree's obvious powers by claiming he could not speak before tasting those apples then suggesting that God's not playing fairly by the rules. He assures her,

> ...Doe not believe
> Those rigid threats of Death; ye shall not die;
> How should ye? By the Fruit? It gives you life
> To knowledge: By the Threatener? Look on mee,
> Mee who have touch'd and tasted, yet both
> live.... (684–88)

The rat-a-tat of short questions-and-inarguable-replies carries great rhetorical weight, logical force, and poetic power.

Satan proceeds from these observable facts to sow doubts about Eve's Creator and appeal both to her logic and her vanity.

> Shall that be shut to Man, which to the Beast
> Is open? or will God incense his ire

> For such a petty trespass, and not praise
> Rather your dauntless virtue? (691–94)

In other words, won't God be impressed that you are willing to dare death by reaching for something which "might
lead/To happier life, knowledge of Good and Evil" (696–
97)? He leads her into a moral syllogism. Knowing what
evil is should allow her still greater insight into the nature
of things, both good and evil.

> ...if what is evil
> Be real, why not known, since easier shunnd?
> God therefore cannot hurt ye, and be just;
> Not just, not God. (697–701)

He sums up by "trash-talking" the Creator, He whom Eve
will soon learn to call "our great Forbidder":

> Why then was this forbid? Why, but to awe,
> Why but to keep ye low and ignorant,
> His worshippers. (703–5)

Satan's own wounded pride seems to be inspiring his proclaimed concern for Eve here; he, too, was recently required to "worship" that Almighty Being. His pride drives
him to pique hers; it is an effort on his part to find a com-
panion in hurt.

He cleverly ends his appeal by seeming to quote pro-
phetically, if unwittingly, from St. Paul; he assures her

> ...that in the day
> Ye eat thereof, your eyes shall seem as clear,
> Yet are but dim, yet perfectly be then
> Open'd and clear'd. (705–8)

The powers that Satan ascribes to the Tree, Paul of course
will ascribe to Faith in Christ (1 Cor 13:12). Milton is plant-
ing, even at the very instant of the Fall, the clear reminder
of God's later redemptive intervention in human affairs
through his Son. He promises to counteract the very Fall
Eve is about to cause before it even happens. Milton takes
that brief moment from Genesis and loads it with his knowledge of New Testament writings and thought. Indeed, one

might call this a daring piece of theology, that without our Fall mankind could not have been rendered even more perfect by Christ's later sacrifice. This theological notion is termed *felix culpa*—the "fortunate fall." Milton prepares us for the idea in the opening lines of the epic where he assures us that after the "loss of Eden" will come "a Greater Man" who will "restore us and regain the blissful seat" (I. 4–5). He pens a literary creation that is, like so much we have examined in this book, every bit worthy of theological analysis as those early, founding documents to which we ascribe definitive and sole authority.

Satan's words are, in any case, irresistible. If we, who know the consequences of her choice, find his arguments persuasive, it is all the easier to sympathize with Eve, for whom this constitutes a first encounter with such rhetorical guile. Milton even concedes that "in her ears the sound/Yet rung of his persuasive words, impregn'd/With Reason, to her seeming, and with Truth" (736–38). Satan speaks true, and much of his argument at least seems full of reason, a gift which modern politicians have not lost. It is a matter of mere minutes before Eve yields, yielding not only to disobedience but to self-indulgence and to a lack of self-discipline: "Greedily she ingorg'd without restraint..." (791). The results of primal sin are huge; she "knew not eating Death."

Milton has the immense and consoling doctrinal recognition that the fall would lead to that "one greater man" who will "restore us" (I. 4–5). For Golding and Tennyson there is less reason and optimism. In *In Memoriam*, Tennyson contemplates such a possibility, as he reflects the new spirit of evolution that was in the air, ten years before Darwin.

> The solid earth whereon we tread
> In tracts of fluent heat began,
> And grew to seeming-random forms,

The seeming prey of cyclic storms,
Till at the last arose the man;
Who throve and branch'd from clime to clime,
The herald of a higher race,
And of himself in higher place,
If so he type this work of time.... (Poem CXVIII, 8–16)

He suggests that man was the product of the whole evolutionary process; imperfect as man was, he could still represent a promise of a better species to come. The poet urges mankind to

Arise and fly
The reeling Faun, the sensual feast;
Move upward, working out the beast,
And let the ape and tiger die. (25–29)

The last line's reference to "ape and tiger" is a subtle reference to the poem's earlier definition of nature as "red in tooth and claw." Tennyson here looks forward, fondly, to the possibility that humans might somehow evolve beyond our inherited role in nature's savage scheme of things and grow ourselves out of that vicious and violent inheritance. He looks to on-going evolution as a possible path to our species' improvement. Golding, the product of a cruel and violent century, holds out no such hope. Neither man had the comfort of firm and absolute Christian doctrine upon which Milton could confidently rely.

　　Putting both his and modern geneticists' hopes aside, it is Milton's business in the remainder of Book IX to explore the far less hopeful consequences of Eve's act. It should come as no surprise that much of Eve's transformation "predicts" the sorts of sin, passion, and moral disruption that we have seen in many of the flawed characters of literature we've previously examined. Once she devours that fruit, she commences a speech which, Milton notes, is "to her self" (794). We are witnessing the birth of narcissism. It should come as no surprise that, like her Tempter, she addresses the plant itself, not its maker. "O Sovran, virtuous, precious of all trees" is her humble apostrophe; she promises that every morning "due praise shall tend thee;" at last, she performs "low reverence" (835). From the mazy folds of *her* selfishness comes idol-worship.

The second god of her idolatry is one that we have heard praised by the Wife of Bath: "experience." Eve praises that habit as her "Best guide; not following thee, I had remained/In ignorance" (808–9). Like Chaucer's God-ignoring and self-indulgent woman, Eve lowers her eyes from God and substitutes personal encounters with her world. Both poets see that a reliance on experience is evil. Though we moderns envy the Wife her distinct individuality, her literary creator means to condemn her, especially her insistence that she would rely on her own experience even if, she says, "noon other auctoritee" existed. We feel her as a distinct, very "modern" individual, but to Chaucer she is a distinctly fallen one. We saw her ability to ignore or misapprehend the Bible's strictures and guidance, which makes her a direct descendent of Milton's Eve. The Wife had only God's Word available to her and chose to ignore or misunderstand it; Eve has the Writer of that very Word Himself available, and yet disobeys Him.

We moderns of course are taught to value experience as both informative and shaping. We scorn the withdrawn life. We honor engagement with the world. And our reverence for science has, for many, displaced the words of the Bible because we consider them embedded in an impossibly obsolete understanding of the universe. It is this respect for experience which David Hume, mentioned earlier, brought to British and European thought. As Baxter writes, "Hume's empiricism [proposed] that all knowledge be based on experience." Golding's take on "The Fall" is, as we saw, eloquent testimony to this modern, scientifically inspired, and progressive view of things. He, like Baxter, is an indirect disciple of Hume. But that knowledge is not Eve's aim. Her genuinely *unprincipled* commitment is purely selfish, purely sensual and amoral.

During this digression we have been not only disparaging Eve but also neglecting her—never a recommended move when dealing with such a new and assertive woman. For, like the Wife, Eve becomes obsessed with appearances and with her behavior around men. "But to Adam in what sort/Shall I appear?" She realizes immediately that looks can be a means to power. "Shall I to him make known/ As yet my change...or...keep the odds of Knowledge in my power/Without Copartner" (816–21)? Like the Wife of Bath, she is drawn to sovereignty in marriage. On that longing, the Wife has built an entire marital career. For Eve, fortunately, it is but a momentary temptation, but for that moment she seriously considers it. She wonders whether her new knowledge might help

> more to draw his Love
> And render me more equal and perhaps
> A thing not undesirable, sometime
> His superior. For inferior who is free? (822–26)

This longing for power reminds us in turn of Lady Macbeth. True, Lady Macbeth never wants to displace her man, but she does intend to use him as her means to advancement. She urges him on against Duncan, for "To be more than what you are/You would be so much more the man" (I.vii.50–51). She poses Eve's key fallen insight: to be inferior is to circumscribe one's freedom. In each case, power and status are the women's yardsticks to genuine human worth, a view that is the product of our evil, fallen natures, habits and evaluations. These three literary women, Lady Macbeth, the Wife of Bath, and Eve (their "general Mother") have yet to learn, though, what

Herbert's collared man recognizes at the end of his meditation, that a life of service, of recognized "inferiority" is
indeed deeply satisfying, deeply gratifying.

Milton's analysis of Eve's new self is, for me, the poem's
most important business. Book IX's remaining 350 lines
concentrate on Eve's return to Adam and her process of
convincing him to complete the fall. The journey to evil
and death is soon completed. There are powerful moments, such as the sight of Adam's "astonishment" at the
sight of Eve.

> …Horror chill
> Ran through his veins and all his joints relax'd;
> From his slack hand The Garland wreath'd for Eve
> Down drop'd, all the faded Roses shed. (890–93)

Again, one would search Genesis in vain for such a scene
or encounter, but Milton the powerful poet creates one
that sounds like the very thing that should have happened.
In the last century or so, sadly, Milton has largely been
relegated to graduate school English study. There was a
time, however, when his version of things would be as well
known and loved as, and its theology more deeply revered
than, Dickens' Scrooge; that is another testimony to the
power of artistic creation to complement, perhaps even
displace, what the fervently faithful prefer to set aside, or
elevate, in a special compartment called Holy.

Adam, in another lovely touch, feels so drawn to Eve,
"flesh of my flesh" (914), that his love drives him to share
Eve's fate, welcoming even death. Milton soon ends this
tragic epic with the sad, resigned reflection that, after
their shared fall,

> Thus they in mutual accusation spent
> The fruitless hours [nice pun there on that fatal fruit],
> but neither self-condemning
> And of their vain contest appear'd no end. (1186–89)

Perhaps it is no coincidence that Golding, though his paleo-anthropological tack is miles removed from Milton's doctrinal drama, ends his novel with the same hopeless prediction: "he could not see if the line of darkness had an ending."

Works Cited

Baxter, Stephen. *Ages in Chaos: James Hutton and the Discovery of Deep Time*. New York: Forge, 2006.

Golding, William. *The Inheritors*. New York: Harvest, 1955.

Milton, John. *Paradise Lost and Paradise Regained*. Ed. Christopher Ricks. New York: Signet, 1968.

6

George Bernard Shaw

Christ's Kingdom in Imperial Britain

I n jumping two centuries from Milton's paradise to George Bernard Shaw's capitalist Britain, we confront the distinctly modern thought of an Irish expatriate, a dedicated socialist, and a fervent but flexible agnostic. The shock may not be as enormous as one might expect, however. Though Shaw reveled in his iconoclasm, and his very long life was in truth one long wrestle primarily with social ills, an equally strong interest lay in religion's flawed doctrines and institutional dead-weight. While he was deeply aware of the Christian gospels' good heart, he still saw the established church as far too cooperative in the system's legal and conventional impediments to his most vital cause—Great Britain's social and economic improvement, particularly the alleviation of the plight of the poor.

This socially committed side of Shaw is crucial to an appreciation of his specific and deep engagement with Christian doctrine; from that real interest it is possible to perceive its relevance to the wider social and economic world he observed and criticized. Indeed, Shaw felt seriously enough about the ills of that world and his obligation to correct them that he wielded a large and vibrant pen. He composed long, witty, articulate prefaces to many of his plays. His goal in doing so was to make clear to the engaged reader—a much larger audience than one theatre could hold—the probingly social or astutely economic points that each play was trying to make. He wrote to be read as well as watched. He admits, in his Preface to

Mrs. Warren's Profession, "I have spared no pains to make known that my plays are built to induce...intellectual interest...[and] humane concern." He was determined that he would "at last persuade even London to take its conscience and its brains with it when it goes to the theatre" (*Plays Unpleasant*, 185).

Shaw's topics were always daring, often challenging. For one thing, he was an ardent feminist. Many of his plays featured strong, independent and assertive women. A particularly eye-opening example of a daring treatment of such a woman was *Mrs. Warren's Profession*. The play was so controversial that the censor—the Lord Chamberlain—banned it. It dared to present sympathetically the life of, to be blunt, a whorehouse madam. More, with characteristic Shavian bravado, that daring play makes the case for her as a specimen of economic success, for her rejecting a proper moral life which would have ended in her death due to the unhealthful conditions working in a white lead factory. His Preface insists that his main character's "Defense of herself...is valid and unanswerable. But it is no defense at all of the vice which she organizes.... Though it is quite natural and right for Mrs. Warren to choose, what is according to her lights, the least immoral alternative, it is nonetheless immoral of society to offer such alternatives" (201–2). Typical of Shaw, he moves a moral or social outcast to center stage, to make a deeper and unanswerable criticism of the economic ways of Britain's social, economic and often imperial world. Such a world Shaw makes it his usual business to portray.

An Imperial Digression

Yes, Shaw is particularly useful for us, for he was writing at what historically was the height of British imperial glory, that empire upon which "the sun never set." Shakespeare wrote for a nascent English kingdom, Christian in spirit and belief. Shaw, in contrast, speaks directly and angrily about the effect of imperial policies and burdens; further, he does so in ways that recall for me Jesus' enraged frustrations with the Roman *imperium*. Contemporary theologians and archeologists, and the Jesus Seminar in particular, with Professor Dominic Crossan in the vanguard, have taken the lead in investigating the life and life style of Judean peasants, the class from which Jesus sprang. They have performed invaluable service in bringing Jesus, in the truest scholarly sense, down to earth. We have learned about village life, economic relations, and the permeating reach of the powers-that-were in first-century Galilee. In that process, they have articulated, in addition, a highly negative take on the evil policies of Rome's "domination system," an *imperium* which made of Jesus just one more faceless victim (or so they thought).

In this matter, Shaw's free spirit seems to bring out the iconoclastic humor in me. Let me entertain a daring suggestion, one that may in fact challenge the attitude of some Seminarians. Perhaps Rome was not all bad. It did, after all, produce what was for its time a revolutionarily efficient and far-flung system of roads; it encouraged communication and facilitated travel. The 1975 film, *The Life of Brian*, provides a hilarious, memorable, and not wholly inaccurate catalogue of "what the Roman Empire has ever done for us"—things like aqueducts, education, roads, and sanitation. Above all, "they like to keep order—they're the only ones who could in a place like this."

Perhaps in its effort to emphasize Jesus' role as a social activist, the Seminar may have stressed too much the evils of the system that executed him. I would at least insist on a wider, complementary perspective: on the whole, the Empire did produce an undeniable level of safety—security imposed over a vast territorial expanse. Furthermore, the establishment of authority under Augustus, the *Pax*

Romana, after decades of republican chaos and civil war, did bring, in its train, undeniable intellectual successes. True, a master of oratory and philosophy like Cicero lived during, and was ultimately a victim of, that chaos, but with the Augustan peace poets like Ovid and Horace arose, along with the master of epic poetry, Virgil. In his epic poem *The Aeneid*, the ghost of Aeneas' father appears to the future Romans in the underworld and predicts the virtues that Rome is destined to proclaim and practice. The prophecy proved remarkably astute and prescient, as the virtues remembered are indeed what Richard Jenkyns in *The Legacy of Rome* calls "its sterner arts of conquest and good government" (iii).

Moreover, may I suggest that the great literature Rome was starting to produce—inspired, admittedly, by the superior Greek literary culture she inherited—may in turn have established, *and* made more accessible, impressive models for later writers to emulate? It was a time of intellectual and literary ferment. Borg has addressed this matter, pointing out the likelihood that the four gospels, composed over a period of maybe thirty years, were created for the relatively small group of seven or eight thousand new adherents. He calls it "an impressive literary production from such a small group" (188). Bart Ehrman, the James A. Gray Distinguished Professor at the University of North Carolina at Chapel Hill, concurs, noting, "There was in fact an extraordinarily wide range of literature being produced, disseminated, read, and followed by the early Christians, quite unlike anything the Roman pagan world had ever seen" (23). Naturally the new faith's fervor is ultimately responsible for that explosion, but the ease and efficiency of communication, as well perhaps a higher regard for literary creations which the lively spirit of the times served to spread, deserve some credit as well.

After all, it was not many years later that the faith had the four gospels in place, if not yet in their final canonical selection and order, along with many Pauline letters assembled for handy access by the growing ranks of the newly faithful. Roman custodial care preserved respect for the Septuagint, though it had been initiated in the third century BCE. Origen was still commissioning additional translations in 235 CE, a tribute to the continuing tradition of Old Testament scholarship in the territories under Roman control. I have to wonder whether such a phenomenon as the Pentecost, whether an historical or simply a symbolic moment of missionary commitment, would even have been possible without the efficient communications which the Empire promoted among the newly formed, deeply evangelical and multi-lingual communities.

Furthermore, the speed of communication, the capacity for rapid dissemination of thought and "news" that those roads allowed, may indeed have contributed to the eventual spread of the gospel. Today's internet demonstrates frighteningly how any one individual's thoughts and reports can explode into the realm of ideas and arenas of action; Roman roads were its brick-and-brick predecessor.

Speaking of a literary tradition, Mark writes with a firm and sophisticated sense of architecture, and with a remarkable command of metaphor that is far more ingenious and subtle than has been previously acknowledged. Bishop Spong, in his *Jesus for the Non-Religious,* has noted, for example, that the gospel's use of a series of "restored eyesight" miracles are intended not as reportage, but as "signs of the in-breaking kingdom." They reveal Jesus "opening the eyes of those who are blind so that they might see their deepest identity" (84). Similarly, Luke's admired powers of narrative may also have been inspired by the higher standards of literary creation that the peace of the Augustan consolidation might have encouraged. Anyone with a feel for powerful literature can hardly fail to be impressed at the way in which Luke adds new dialogue in the service of a radically modified theology in his transformation of Mark's already dramatic and poignant Passion chapters. Mark's Jesus gives a final cry of dereliction; Luke replaces that despair with serial assertions of loving control. Mark's two mute criminals now speak; one of them earns paradise through his spoken confirmation of Jesus as the Christ. Luke's thief has a far better understanding than Mark's singularly slow-witted disciples. Luke provides one of the very earliest examples of the power of fictional religion to revise, shape and proclaim fundamental Christian doctrine.

Now, allow me one further and still more daring suggestion. Who knows whether, in earlier Mediterranean history, another man *like* Jesus may have lived, spoken out, and been similarly throttled? Suppose that, in this earlier case, the word of his exploits and his message never got sufficient notice, or did not resonate with the intellectual or religious culture of the era sufficiently to spread and take root. The conditions of the Jews under the Babylonians were far worse, exiled as they were, than under Rome's unquestionably iron fist—stern, unwilling to compromise, and systematically harsh. Without suggesting some quaint notion of a World Spirit operating over time, it does seem that the world under Augustus' reign was ready for a concept like a savior and a resurrection. Perhaps human history, in conjunction with an undeniably remarkable human being, and the new availability of sophisticated literary traditions, all came together to forge what proved to be a lasting miraculous event.

Shaw on Christian Activism

Major Barbara offers yet another sample of English literature that takes as its subject ideas that derive from what we may call the proto-orthodox Christian doctrine, which was progressively set forth in the four formative gospels (six if we include the ones called Q and Thomas). Our twenty-first-century take is informed by an improved and dispassionate scholarly consensus, which is coming to a less sentimental, more worldly image of Jesus. We are realizing how deeply committed Jesus was to seeking justice for his community. Even allowing for the successive gospels' growing and changing propagandistic purposes, it seems clear that the actual, historical Jesus was a peripatetic preacher and, probably, healer. He traveled continually through the Galilean villages and countryside. He sat down to eat with all manner of people, a habit for which he was roundly condemned by his Jewish betters, men unalterably committed to strict kosher practice.

Borg, among others, supports the view that much of Jesus' work on earth was indeed focused *on* the earth, on the here and now. Jesus may have had some apocalyptical visions, but it would seem that most of his efforts were, like those of many Jewish prophets, directing God's proclaimed passion for justice toward the affairs of our world. As our faith has evolved and adapted over two millennia, this worldly focus on what we might call social activism has been at best inconsistent. The notion of an eternal reward, not to mention that of sacrificial atonement, has often gotten the lion's share of theological—and behavioral—attention, especially in Pentecostal American traditions. Still, scholarship by Borg and others reveals this to be a misplaced emphasis. "Jesus' mission and message were not about 'heaven,' not about how to attain a blessed afterlife" (143).

To amplify Borg's point, consider the secondary status granted to the activism of good works as reflected in a single inserted punctuation point—a mere comma—in the usual versions of the "Lord's Prayer." In the Episcopal Book of Common Prayer, the crucial petition reads, "Thy kingdom come, thy will be done,/On earth as it is in Heaven." This

sing-song attempt in the second line to achieve a neat rhetorical balance is poor theology, and it encourages sloppy
thinking. The placement of the comma confuses the issue
profoundly. The prayer as we have it humbly asks, rightly
of course, for the arrival of God's kingdom here amongst
us, and that we do His will. Ah, but it then *equates* its earthly
achievement with its enactment in heaven.

Who are we to point out to God how to run heaven?
Yet this is what the rhythm created by the punctuation proclaims. The key, the intention of the prayer, is instead to
ask Him to bring down to earth the perfect justice which
He by definition "does" endlessly in His realm. The request therefore should read and be punctuated this way:
"Thy kingdom come, thy will be done *on earth* (just like
it is in heaven)." That's what Jesus urged his hearers: the
attainment on earth of the godly Realm toward which his
parables pointed. As Borg notes, Jesus in his ministry "became a passionate advocate of God's passion for justice"
(134).

It is this kind of activism Shaw urges in most of his plays,
which draw their audience's attention to the social ills of
the world they share with the playwright. In *Major Barbara*,
it is the eminently worldly version of the petition—that
God's kingdom come on earth—that the play's hero, the
title character, voices at its climax. It is very nearly a demand that, daringly, makes God dependent on *us* for that
kingdom's achievement.

Major Barbara (with a saintly assist)

To fully appreciate the climactic moment of *Major Barbara*,
we require one further digression, a brief exploration of
Shaw's *Saint Joan* (1923), a play explicitly and entirely devoted to a religious figure. For an agnostic, Shaw is endlessly fascinated by religion and the various phenomena it
has generated. As one might expect of an iconoclast tak-

ing on a massive institution, Shaw's Preface to *Saint Joan* shows little patience with the Catholic Church. Shaw has a very clear-eyed sense of its many deficiencies. Its flawed system for choosing popes is just one example: "It appears that the successive steps of selection and election are of the superior by the inferior (the cardinal vice of democracy) with the result that great popes are as rare and accidental as great kings" (56). He goes on to remark that, in the Church's long history, "All the great orders arose from dissatisfaction with the priests:...the Franciscans with priestly snobbery,... the Dominicans with priestly laziness..., the Jesuits with priestly apathy and ignorance and indiscipline" (53–54). He respects some of what the institution has produced, but especially admires the occasions when individuals rise up against the stultifying effects of ingrained magisterial habit.

Shaw's impatience with institutional authority resembles, as suggested earlier, that of Jesus, who had what proved to be a dangerously low regard for the Jewish authorities of his day. His angry behavior in the Temple, days before his execution, is what Borg has called an act of political theatre. Whether the claim is strictly accurate, the event itself has the ring of historical fact. Similarly, Shaw, like his fellow Socialists, was carrying on a constant battle both on stage and in print with the money changers of his day—the financiers and corporate giants of the British establishment. Shaw saw those bodies standing in the way of genuine social justice. As the lead character Andrew Undershaft, munitions manufacturer and millionaire, proclaims in *Major Barbara,* "*I* am the government of your country" (119). Even today, we see corporate influence in our American affairs of state, particularly those driving the nation in military, indeed imperial, directions.

It is also consistent with Shaw's contrariness that, in *St. Joan,* he puts what are perhaps the wisest and most caring words of any person in the play into the mouth of the Inquisitor assigned to Joan's case. Shaw loves to subvert audience expectations and comfortable prejudices. Here he seems to be counting on his British, Protestant audience's presumably low regard for the Catholic Inquisition, that cruel and doctrinaire institution that so often proved fatal to suspected heretics. Then he surprises us. The Inquisitor's advice to his fellow court members is admirably loving and charitable. It is, indeed, deeply Christian:

> Though the work I have to do may seem cruel to those who do not know how much more cruel it would be to leave it undone, I would go to the stake myself sooner than do it if I did not know its righteousness, its necessity, its essential mercy.... Anger is a bad counselor: cast out anger. Pity is sometimes worse: cast out pity. But do not cast out mercy. (*Saint Joan*, 167)

As the Preface explains, the church's "method was not cruelty's for cruelty's sake but for the salvation of Joan's soul" (53).

Here Shaw also makes the incisive point that "Joan believed that the saving of her soul was her own business" (53). He sees in her a proto-Protestant, a remarkably modern and particularly self-sufficient woman. In his reverence for her, Shaw makes a case for her sort of radically original thinking; it's the same original habit of mind he sees in Socrates and in other imaginative thinkers. Indeed, his definition of a genius fits very well my sense of the man Jesus: "a person who, seeing further and probing deeper than other people, has a different set of ethical valuations from theirs, and has energy enough to give effect to this extra vision and its valuations in whatever manner best suits his or her specific talents" (20). In *Reimagine the World*, Brandon Scott reinforces Shaw's insight: "Jesus the story teller seems to me closer to a poet. The activist will always be dissatisfied with the poetic vision, but change comes about because a creative individual has that vision" (138). Joan is a Christian saint in that adjective's truest and most activist sense of the word.

In *Major Barbara,* Shaw finds fault even with a sect whose good works he applauds—the Salvation Army. Here was a sect that was at least genuinely activist. It was taking Jesus' gospel into the streets, seeking constantly to alleviate the sufferings of the indigent and unemployed, Britain's version of the broken nobodies whose plight Jesus himself most deeply felt. *Major Barbara* declares Shaw's deep admiration for the Army's mission to the poor, but it voices just as clearly his profound rejection of its institutional procedures and financial dependency. The Army, Shaw shows, ultimately *needs* those same powers, not mere money-changers, who rule Britain—distillers and arms merchants, for starters.

Shaw's heroine, Barbara Undershaft, though born to the manner of the rich and privileged, turns her back on that comfortable and self-satisfied upbringing. A social revolutionary, she throws in her lot with the Army's daily work in London's mean and wintry streets. She has an instinctive commonality of interests with the Jesus whom we sense behind—and sometimes directly behold in—the gospels. Young, assertive Major Barbara shows a devout double determination. She wants to bring God's people back to faith, naturally, but she is equally devoted to lifting up London's down-and-out. It's a dedication she pursues through the generous provision of milk, bread, treacle, and prayer, as well as her own irresistible assertiveness. She learns soon enough, however, that even those instruments of salvation have to be compensated. She finds she must devote far too much of her energy to daily collections of the cold cash (literally) that her good works demand.

Her strength and devotion, like those of most of
Shaw's heroines, excite our admiration, but her father
finds fault with her approach to perfecting the world. The
play becomes, in effect, a debate between her Christian
activism and his industrial-strength path to economic paradise. Andrew Undershaft demonstrates—and his daughter quickly learns how right he is—that all her efforts will
go to waste until society's economic system is repaired.
She comes to see that she has been luring the poor to the
gospel through *food*; she is brought to the realization that
what these suffering people most fundamentally need is a
reliable *income*. Only with that can they become self-sufficient, earn their own food, and create a life of self-respect.
It is this world of personal economic sufficiency that her
father has provided through, ironically, his munitions factory, his implements of war.

Jesus in his parables and Shaw in his play both see and
condemn the harsh social and economic system under
which the world's poor and needy suffered. For Jesus it
was the natural operation of the expanding, cruel, and
morally arrogant Roman empire; Shaw sees with the same
eyes, but he chooses a representative of the very institution
that was the engine of an expansive, capitalist British empire to be his spokesman. Both men saw how their respec-
tive imperial oppressors worked. As we shall see, however,
Shaw is more optimistic than Jesus about a better result.
Also unlike Jesus, he died peacefully in his bed at age 94.

When Barbara visits her father's munitions works, she
finds the place, as her fiancé says, "horribly, immorally, unanswerable perfect" (123). It is there that she rises to the
new, distinctly non-doctrinal yet more deeply Christian
insight that is the play's climax. Her exultant declaration
voices its essential redemptive message: "I have got rid of
the bribe of bread. I have got rid of the bribe of heaven."
No, she insists, "Let God's work be done for its own sake:

the work he had to create us to do because it cannot be done except by living men and women." Perhaps most blasphemously she declares, "When I die let him be in debt, not I in his" (147).

In phrasing her vision this way, she comes close to what John Dominic Crossan terms Jesus' vision of "collaborative eschatology"—that is, the "collaboration between the divine and the earthly." Only when the intended recipients of the gospel message are "full-fed" creatures can they have the self-confidence and integrity to come to God on their own terms. How daring—and very modern—to reorder the universe to make God subservient to us! As Crossan observed, "God isn't going to do it without you." Indeed, Barbara would insist he *cannot!* Hers is a God of action, dedicated to making the world better. If "Thy kingdom" is to "come," it must be worldly men and women who bring it to fruition. Such a declaration is the kind of daring message about Christ's purpose that Jesus Seminarians are perhaps most apt to appreciate and revere.

While Jesus' words were spoken in a context of imperial suppression and cruelty, Shaw wrote at a time when there were new democratic stirrings, traceable to the Enlightenment and the principles to which it first gave voice. There was a sense that humanity *could* achieve progress—both social justice and financial security—here on earth. There was a new confidence that society could move, if not toward heaven on earth, at least in the direction of a society where the individual could imagine a real if pale replica of such a paradise. To that extent, Shaw is working from a wholly different social and philosophical context than was Jesus of Nazareth. But the work to which he has Barbara commit at the play's end is far closer to the kinds of emphasis that, we now are coming to realize, the historical Jesus also voiced. At the end of *Major Barbara*, the play's heroine invokes a kingdom of god that, while

not visible to naked imperial eyes, might serve to give another empire's victims—the British and European social
and economic system—a certifiable sense of self.

Shaw, an articulate and probing social activist and
analyst, is here proposing a modern *and achievable* better
world. At the end of his preface he makes a characteristically proud assertion about his play, a proclamation the
arrogance of which does not detract from its accuracy:
"This play of mine is both true and inspired." It tackles a
religious subject and makes crucial discoveries about the
Christian mission. He hastens to add, however, that "faith
in it and understanding of it [do not] consist in believing
[it actually happened]" (42). *Major Barbara* is, like all the
stories and poems we have examined in this book, a work
of fiction, yet it, like them, is as powerful, incisive, and
inspired as those stories and injunctions contained and
proclaimed in the four gospels.

For the broken nobodies who were the usual victims of
the Roman Empire's efficient cruelties, Jesus articulated a
godly kingdom. As Scott suggests, "Jesus told parables to
let people in on his experience of God. [Parables] were his
way of making God available to them" (31). Jesus was always careful to avoid painting that kingdom too precisely.
He was either being coy or profound when he warned
folks, "You won't be able to observe the coming of God's
kingdom. People are not going to be able to say, 'Look,
here it is' or 'Over there.'" (Luke 17:20–21).

For Shaw, such a Kingdom stood a greater chance of
being realized. He saw in his day that men and women
were becoming increasingly able to create a just society in
which all might begin to hope they could own a share. To
his mind, Socialism was Christian ethics in action.

Works Cited

Borg, Marcus. *Jesus*. New York: HarperOne, 2006.

Crossan, John Dominic. Interview with John Dart. Westar Fall Meeting. October 15, 2010.

Ehrman, Bart D. *Misquoting Jesus*. New York: HarperOne, 2005.

Jenkyns, Richard. *The Legacy of Rome: A New Appraisal*. Oxford University Press, 1992.

Scott, Bernard Brandon. *Reimagine the World*. Salem, OR: Polebridge, 2001.

Shaw, George Bernard. *Plays Unpleasant*. New York: Penguin, 1958.

———. *Pygmalion* and *Major Barbara*. New York: Bantam, 1992.

———. *St. Joan. Collected Plays with their Prefaces*. New York: Dodd, Mead, 1972.

Spong, John Shelby. *Jesus for the Non-Religious*. New York: HarperOne, 2007.

7

William Faulkner's "Barn Burning"

A Modern, Secular Vision of Community

William Faulkner's ideal community shares many features with Shakespeare's even though it arrives over three centuries later. In "Barn Burning," set in the fictional county of Yopknapatawpha in the post Civil War South, the young lad Colonel Sartoris Snopes (Sarty) has led thus far an unexamined life of tribal loyalty—the unquestioning allegiance demanded by his harsh, unfeeling, self-regarding patriarch of a father, Abner. The story dramatizes the boy's slowly-dawning realization that he must escape from that harsh, nomadic world and instead affirm and join a society governed by law and justice.

In turning to this modern American writer we turn to what is for all intents and purposes a religion-free—certainly dogma-free—society. It is true that in many of his tales of the South there are church-going people; Sunday attendance is part of their culture. But here, it's as if Faulkner has stripped out any specific doctrinal matters or religious practices and focused more strictly on a secular but secure and harmonious social order. If the words of the gospel are spoken, and in this tale they are not, it's merely a verbal veneer. What we witness in this tale is a community which seeks to elevate and achieve coherence and stability through an array of secular, agreed-upon social habits of thought and behavior. Law replaces creed, and deferential and disciplined behavior becomes a stand-in for both worship and dogma. Such a strategy serves to verify that, thanks to humane ethical practices and a firm reliance on the role of law to create order, society can lead the good life without specific reliance on religious dogma.

The story walks us through Sarty's dawning awareness, and eventual rejection, of his father's system of values and way of life. As it opens, Abner is being tried in court for burning down a neighbor's barn. He is found innocent only because the judge has no direct evidence, only a hear-say conversation between Abner and the victim, a Mr. Harris, at which Sarty was present. The kindly judge combines strict law with merciful application of it; he is "troubled" (5) at having to question the boy, a point on which even Harris concurs. The freed Abner moves his family and their belongings to a new shack in a new county, where they again will be tenant farmers, this time, however, to a highly civilized and well-to-do man, Major De Spain. Sarty hopes deep down his father will settle down and become part of the community, but his father's first deed on arriving at his new master's estate subverts those hopes. Abner asserts his primitive independence by first stepping in horse dung and then smearing it on De Spain's splendid rug. When Abner subsequently fails to clean it properly, and in fact ruins it with hot lye when told to clean it, De Spain charges him a portion of his anticipated crop yield.

Abner takes his new boss to court and gets the fine reduced. That he can do so shows that, in this orderly polity, justice is democratic; it is available to "all the people." A lowly tenant can sue the lord of the manor. But Abner, always the outsider, remains unsatisfied; he undertakes another pyromaniac revenge. Sarty runs to warn De Spain, with the result that his father is shot and killed. On a symbolic level, Sarty has displaced his father and become a free individual, committed to an entirely new set of communal values. It is significant for this study that Faulkner turns to other literary systems of value, not Christian, in an attempt to intensify the resonance of his tale. The story is included in this study of the evolution of inherited Christian doctrine as a reminder of the ways avowedly Christian tenets continue to shape individual behavior and social relations. Doctrinal ideals continue to hold sway, even when divorced from dogmatic certainty.

For one thing, though he wrote the story in the 1930s, he consciously sets it at the start of a new legal era for the South—the end of the Civil War. Faulkner wants to show a society being born, or at least a young society reaching out to incorporate a hitherto nemesis of that order. He gives the relationships between Sarty and his father genuinely mythic status, fashioning the story on the model of Greek myth—the displacement of the older order of Titans (Chronos) by the younger and more humane God, Zeus. The story therefore traces not just one boy's rejection of his cruel father, but the evolution of society overall from tribe to social compact. Just as Portia's mercy defeats Shylock's strict, harsh, pound-of-flesh justice in *The Merchant of Venice*—and does so in a court of law—here, too, Abner's cold and tribal code of tribal loyalty and vindictiveness is found wanting and replaced by a far more humane set of values, firm but flexible.

Abner's order is cruel and repressive. Sarty is proud of his father's service in the Civil War, but the narrator reminds the reader that he entered that conflict "as a private in the fine old European sense..., giving fidelity to no man or army or flag." He is the sole law in his family, and of all its members (two sons, two daughters, a wife and an aunt), Sarty is the only one to rise up and question his father's cruel dictates and violent behavior. He is also the only character to be given a name, aside from a

brief mention of his mother's. The older brother is un-
thinking and docile; the daughters are lazy and without
wills of their own; the mother is a helpless but pained victim of a loveless marriage, unable to act. The tribe is an
eloquent portrait of a primitive, nomadic lifestyle in sore
need of redemption. Only the aunt, at a crucial moment
when Abner directs his wife to hold Sarty down, tells her
sister to "Let him go. If he don't go, before God, I'll go up
there myself." In Faulkner's mythical realm, this moment
serves as a social revolution, the rejection by its victims of
a timeless—the family clock has not worked in a generation—and endlessly repressive order.

Through Sarty, Faulkner takes a strong stand in be-
half of the same kind of nourishing, ethical civil order
proposed in *Macbeth*. Faulkner posits a secular and rural heaven, invested with values that Shakespeare would
surely have acknowledged, though the dramatist would
have anchored them to a specifically Christian vocabulary. Perhaps it would not be too provincial to suggest
the difference is American in spirit, traceable to Thomas
Jefferson's "Declaration of Independence." At the start of
this founding document, the man who would become the
nation's third president appeals first to "Nature and [only
secondarily]...Nature's God." At its end he addresses that
God as a "Judge." In so doing, he identifies no specific
Christian doctrine; rather, he seems intent on celebrating
his era's Enlightenment ideals of reason and law. Jefferson
proposes, and Faulkner dramatizes, the way to found a nation, not a religious faith.

Faulkner invents a more secular and far less doctrinal
order than Shakespeare's, a world where the rule of law,
yoked with a merciful interpretation of it, is the supreme
guarantor of a civil order. Christian doctrine is never articulated; nevertheless, its ethical principles are implicit in
the humane social order Faulkner paints. Macbeth unwill-

ingly cuts himself off from a moral and humane order that he knows to be "right," and he just as rightly foresees the human and psychological consequences of that divorce. Sarty, on the other hand, learns to *ally* himself with the humane order he encounters, one that is based on justice, the law, rules, and self-discipline. The process costs him his family, but he gains a restorative community. At journey's end, day is dawning and Sarty walks off resolutely from what remains of his family: "He did not look back" (27). Sarty reverses Macbeth's trajectory.

The new world the lad embraces is much like Duncan's healthful and organic one. Major De Spain is a humane, forceful and well-regarded landlord. Like Shakespeare's medieval Scotland, Faulkner's rural world is distinctly feudal in both its social and agricultural operations. Indeed, it is no coincidence that much of the South about which Faulkner writes was, in fact, settled by eighteenth- and nineteenth-century Scottish immigrants. Sarty senses instinctively that this order is marked by security and justice the minute he and Abner encounter the fence surrounding Major De Spain's gorgeous mansion. Like the banquet scene in *Macbeth,* the moment when Sarty beholds the mansion becomes an artistically crucial and intellectually complex enactment of the work's defining theme and world-view. Each scene proclaims its creator's defining message. For Sarty, the aristocratic home is a personal revelation.

> They walked beside a fence massed with honeysuckle and Cherokee roses and came to a gate swinging open between two brick pillars and now, beyond a sweep of drive, he saw the house for the first time and at that instant he forgot his father and the terror and despair both.... "They are safe from him" [Sarty thinks to himself]." People whose lives are a part of this peace and dignity are beyond his touch." (10–11)

That fence image is vital to Faulkner's point, both literally and metaphorically. Literally, unlike the fences Sarty
has known heretofore, which Abner regularly uses for
firewood, De Spain's is woven with honeysuckle and roses;
it delights the senses, of both nose and eye. At its center
stands that open gate, a clever fusion of restrained order—"good fences make good neighbors"—and gracious
welcome. The beauty of the place echoes Banquo's paean
of praise for Macbeth's comparably marvelous castle.

Sarty's instinctive simile upon beholding the mansion
is even more revealing: "Hits big as a courthouse" (11). His
pronunciation reminds us of the Snopes's lack of refinement, but the noun is key: it shows an instantaneous and
awed realization. This place's "peace and dignity" spring
from a profound respect for law, a force Sarty has subcon-
sciously admired, though as a tribal member he has been
taught to hate it. And it is not only the outside of the house
that seduces Sarty. When he enters—just before Abner
soils that wonderful rug—he's also taken by the wealth
within: "deluged as though by a warm wave by a suave
turn of carpeted stair and a pendant glitter of chandeliers
and a mute gleam of gold frames" (12). Faulkner subtly
connects the rule of law ("big as a courthouse") with the
possibility of wealth, refinement, luxury. No doubt those
gold frames enclose portraits of relatives and thus declare
the importance of family tradition far more elegantly than
Abner's thinner notion of sticking to one's blood.

These values infuse the entire narrative. For one thing,
in that same mansion Sarty beholds his first womanly
ideal. Unlike his battered and helpless mother, the woman
of the house wears a "gray smooth gown with lace at the
throat and an apron tied at the waist." She is elegant, and
she enters the room "wiping cake or biscuit dough from
her hands" (12–13). This is no idle rich lady but a working woman, responsible for the house's food, which has

always lured the underfed Sarty, underfed both in body and spirit. As in *Macbeth,* sustenance is crucial.

Nourishment is a crucial notion. The opening trial, for instance, is held not in an austere courtroom, but in a general store. "The Store... smelled of cheese" and on its shelves Sarty can see row upon row of canned meats. Faulkner's use of these props serves to reinforce the short story's central notion that justice is indeed healthful. The store to which people come for food is also the place where the community gathers, and it is also the place to which that community comes to see justice carried out. Like the central banquet in Macbeth, the general store symbolizes an ideal, socially nutritive order. Faulkner's is grounded in law and it offers communal sustenance, both bodily and jurisprudential.

The values that define this new world extend even to the narrator. When Abner is found innocent at the opening trial, and the judge firmly suggests he leave the area, he replies with words that are "unprintable." There are such things as social standards and the teller of the tale abides by them. Furthermore, when Abner voices these obscenities the judge replies with restraint: "That'll do." He does not rise to the freed defendant's bait; he does not lower himself to reply in kind. He evinces self-discipline, another key element in the conquest of the tolerant social order over the vindictively tribal.

This model behavior is displayed by Faulkner throughout the story by his use of the concept of a fence, the same fence we saw around the De Spain mansion. He threads it throughout the story in brilliantly imaginative ways. In the country-store trial, the judge calls the boy forward to testify and asks Harris if he really wants him to question Sarty. "'No,' Harris said violently, explosively. 'Get him out of here.'" Harris knows Sarty is a vital witness, but he yields to a higher ethical standard. He sacrifices his chance for a just verdict by deferring to a humane instinct; he "fences" in his desire for revenge and yields to common decency, just as the judge does in reply to Abner's harsh attack.

Much the same thing occurs later, after Abner has destroyed Major De Spain's rug. The owner shows up "trembling, speaking in a shaking voice," but he stops short of violence. Revenge is tempting for De Spain, Harris and the first judge, but all three show restraint. They have mastered the self-discipline that reflects their willing agreement to abide by the dictates of a beneficent ethical and legal order.

That fences are key elements to a healthful order is further confirmed in the new region to which the Snopes family moves. Faulkner notes that mother and aunt have saved money to buy Sarty an axe, which they "present him with at Christmas." It's the story's only reference to a religious holiday, which does give it an extra force, and he now "built pens for the shoat and the cow which were part of his father's contract with the landlord" (18). It's significant that this moment is the only one in the story in which several family members cooperate, and they do so in response to the requirements of a legal document. More significantly still, the axe is being put to constructive use. It was Abner's failure to pen in his pigs on Harris' property that caused the first barn burning and trial.

One further appearance of a fence is similarly meaningful. After the second trial, at which the judge suspends half of Abner's penalty, the father and two brothers gather around a yard in the center of town. Abner produces a sack with crackers and cheese and proceeds to slice the cheese into shares for all three. It is his only moment of sharing, and what is shared is food. The moment builds Sarty's hopes—and our own—for Abner's restorative integration. It goes further when the three do not go immediately home. They gather around a horse lot, "A tall fence upon and along which men stood and sat," and spend the entire afternoon assessing the various horses brought out for sale. Signs are hopeful for Abner's having found a community, gathered together cooperatively on a fence, a society into which he might enter and be accepted. It makes his subsequent relapse into pyromania all the more tragic.

Seeing De Spain's mansion has turned Sarty inside out. He becomes a disciple of the order it declares. So, at the climax, he runs to his "new" father (Major De Spain) to warn him of the fiery revenge his biological father is planning. As he flees the scene, Sarty shouts the rural "Pap, Pap" out of natural, filial concern, but when he hears the rifle shots that he knows are killing that tyrant, he calls out, "Father, father." His new, refined vocabulary confirms his commitment to the new world of order, luxury, peace, security, health and nourishment. Without any religious terminology, young Sarty still declares a profound and now organic relationship to an ideal world not all that different from Shakespeare's.

Work Cited

Faulkner, William "Barn Burning." Pp. 1–27 in *Selected Short Stories of William Faulkner.* New York: Modern Library, 1961.

8

Philip Larkin

A Thoughtful but Skeptical View of Christian Faith

Shakespeare's vision of an ideal kingly commonwealth in *Macbeth* was a deeply healthful and organic one. Faulkner's similarly feudal take on an ideal community governed by justice and order shows that even a modern regional writer describing a simple, rural community finds virtue in those same lasting moral and ethical principles. George Herbert provides a poignant but ultimately orthodox portrait of a profoundly pious, momentarily rebellious Christian priest returning instinctively (or by a long-ingrained) habit of pious conformity to humility and obedience.

The playwright, the story writer and the poet were all writing within, or at least within the gravitational pull of, a traditional Christian context. Each achieves a memorably rendered insight into and version of that conventionally accepted world-view. Philip Larkin, one of two twentieth-century artists we'll examine, might seem at first an unlikely successor to the authors previously discussed. For him, it is pretty evident that god's kingdom has vanished. Indeed, for him, that realm was never realizable, much though we imperfect humans might crave its reassuring embrace.

It might be useful to notice the uses to which the Christian tradition continued to be put as the culture grew increasingly secular and brought increasingly suspicious scrutiny to inherited belief and doctrine during the early twentieth century. The Christian tradition continued as a source of allusions, a literary reservoir, whereby contemporary phenomena could be defined or assessed. One example is William Butler Yeats, the Irish poet. He looked around himself in the 1920s and saw the rise of angry and chaotic political forces, like Communists and Fascists, phenomena which led him to ask a horrific question in his "The Second Coming":

> "What rough beast, its hour come round at last
> Slouches toward Bethlehem to be born?" (20–21)

The dystopian allusion to Jesus in the stable serves to suggest that, according to the poet's vision, two millennia of peace and salvation have had their day and a new, frightening, and monstrous generation was about to gain power and wreak destruction. Yeats uses the Christian birth-narrative to explicate his dangerous world and suggest that the Christian era was closing. Even if modern scholarship has taught us that Bethlehem was not Jesus' actual birthplace, Matthew and Luke's fictional narratives had been granted doctrinal authority by two millennia of cultural consent; the allusion still packs an enormous symbolic wallop.

Like Yeats, the poet T. S. Eliot wrote early poems that subvert Christian motifs in order to express his feelings in response to what he saw his age coming to—despair, loss and displacement. His Bible story of choice is the Matthean tale of the Three Wise Men in his "Journey of the Magi." That visionary trio is of course another revered staple of the Christ story, the full-fledged invention of one gospel—the vibrancy of which is confirmed by Gian Carlo Menotti's miraculous Christmas opera, "Amahl and the Night Visitors," which is itself a fictional accretion that is as theologically pure as the fictional tale it embroiders so wonderfully.

When Eliot tells the story of the Magi's journey, he does not paint it as the coming of the promise of salvation to the world so much as portray it from the view of a dying order. Eliot begins: "A hard coming we had of it,/Just the worst time of year for a journey." From beginning to its end, the three questers are in no celebratory mood. They wonder, "Were we led all that way for a Birth or a Death?" Eliot stands Matthew's story on its head, erasing the hopeful promise of Christ; we see the three thrown into doubt at what they have witnessed. Their speaker confesses that "this Birth was like hard and bitter agony for us" and ends with resignation and despair: "I should be glad of another death." Eliot expresses the new, iconoclastic, modernist take on traditional culture and the inherited stories and beliefs, much of them Christian, which that culture used to revere.

Britain's turn-of-the-century imperial grandeur, about which Shaw wrote and implicitly criticized, was matched across the Channel by "La Belle Epoque," that is, France's "lovely era." Soon, however, all that European luxury and confidence was wiped out by the horrors of trench warfare and by world leaders' seeming inability to end the Great War's carnage. The war's close brought with it the vindictive treatment of Germany, which led to that country's hyper-inflation, which in turn gave rise to Hitler...and Mussolini and Stalin. The political world, in short, provided ample fodder for a widely-held sense that the world was careening out of control. Yeats was not alone in thinking so. The young F. Scott Fitzgerald wrote *This Side of Paradise* in 1920, where he pronounced "all Gods dead, all wars fought, and all faiths in man shaken." It was into this era that Larkin was born.

Larkin's sense of his era's disillusionment, and of his personal inability to relate to the faith he inherited, does not mean that he has no regard for faith. Though his take

is detached and coolly objective, his almost obsessive interest in this subject seems to reflect his quite intense spiritual anomie and despair. Several of his poems do assess
spiritual phenomena and practices he sees around him,
though he rarely addresses any specifically doctrinal matters. He was serious enough about the topic one time to
contemplate, in his unique way, the actual creation of a
faith. His criteria in "Water" (93) tell us a lot:

> If I were called in
> To construct a religion
> I should make use of water.
>
> Going to church
> Would entail a fording
> To dry, different clothes.
>
> My liturgy would employ
> Images of sousing,
> A furious devout drench.
>
> And I should raise in the east
> A glass of water
> Where any-angled light
> Would congregate endlessly.

His vision certainly presupposes the idea of transformation. He admires the miraculous liquid both for its power
to change as well as and its endless internal metamor-
phoses. The multiplicity of angles that "congregate" in
it shoves aside any mention of a human "congregation."
Larkin employs appropriate ecclesiastical terms like "lit-
urgy" or "the east," but his recommendations are curiously
solipsistic. He never mentions any human participants. He
focuses on those ideals of an almost sensory process of intense change, like the "furious devout drench." "Sousing"
even hints at intoxication. More conventionally, he also
sees any journey to church as a way of changing the old
self; the water offers a "fording" to something dry and dif-

ferent. He uses faith as a means to change what we are and thus employs traditional language about religion's purposes. Christianity looks to the east for the "Sun" of God." Larkin's libation, "[raised] in the east" seems restricted to the protean, vitality of liquid—natural renewal, not the Resurrection. If this seems at least hopeful on his part, the stance is rare.

The fact is that generally Larkin is cynical about the possibility of love in this world, and of a *next* one he rejects the very possibility. In "The Old Fools" (196), a depressing response to a visit to an old folks' home, he analyzes quite pitilessly the dissolution that death brings:

> At death you break up: the bits that were you
> Start speeding away from each other for ever
> With no one to see. (13–15)

He foresees no self beyond the grave, though he at least admits that life did once hold out some promise. Of the death toward which those old folks move he says,

> It's only oblivion, true:
> We had it before, but then it was going to end,
> And was all the time merging with a unique endeavour
> To bring to bloom the million-petalled flower
> Of being here. (15–19)

That first oblivion, presumably experienced in the womb or even prior to conception, does promise the many blossoms of possibility, of the potential inherent in simply "being here." That hopeful springtime of possibility echoes the "any-angled water" from "Water." But our second oblivion is the permanent one: Death.

Death is, for Larkin, on a regular and recurring basis, life's ultimate fact. It is an obsession. In "Ambulances" (132) he makes an explicit statement about its prevalence and inevitability (see Appendix). The first stanza ends with the observation that "All streets in time are visited." Employing double entendre, Larkin uses "in time" to mean not only "eventually" but to remind us that we dwell in a universe that is governed by time. We will all watch this unwelcome vehicle come to our door. The fate of that "wild white face" on that stretcher is made clear by the verb "stowed." The person is but a thing to be shelved. That the message goes out to all witnesses is equally clear. The "solving emptiness/That lies under all we do" is Larkin's stark reminder that our daily chores and busy-ness simply conceal temporarily the "nothing" that lurks beneath that activity. That is why the words uttered by the women and children who witness the departure—"poor soul"— are words that in truth "they whisper at their own distress." That distress is that second oblivion lying in wait for us all.

But what about the life that sprang from that first "oblivion" in "The Old Fools"? The second one, the one we all live, which death brings about—that once potentially-glorious "flower of being here"? Surely life, our one life holds promise, yes? Well, alas no. In many of his poems, Larkin insists that that one chance to grow and tend a million petals of joy brings only frustration and failure. One of his most concise poems, "As Bad as a Mile" (125), examines a simple, everyday action brilliantly and with devastating skepticism, using Biblical allusions to do it. He employs images from Genesis to define life as inevitable failure. Here is another writer continuing to mine that vast Biblical reservoir that is our shared heritage—cultural, literary and moral.

> Watching the shied core
> Striking the basket, skidding across the floor
> Shows less and less of luck, and more and more
>
> Of failure spreading back up the arm
> Earlier and earlier, the unraised hand calm,
> The apple unbitten in the hand. (1–6)

The poem, short, deceptively simple and superficially quotidian, is in truth profound. The thoughtful reader, sensitive to that shared Judeo-Christian heritage, sees that the simple act of missing the waste basket when throwing an apple core can be traced back to that first apple in Eden, the moment before it was first "bitten." It was same act which, as Milton shows at great length, brought "all that woe" into the world. Missing the wastebasket is a minor woe, certainly. But Larkin, like Yeats and Eliot, has used a reliable Biblical reference to explain our wider and deeper disabilities.

Larkin cleverly walks us backward through time and shows us a further consequence of that Sin. That "calm hand," motionless before flinging the core, can also be seen as a prophecy of Cain's murder of Abel, seen before it is "raised"—an implicit hint at anger.

> Then the LORD said to Cain... "[If] you do not do
> what is right, sin is crouching at your door; it desires to
> have you, but you must master it." Now Cain said to his
> brother Abel, "Let's go out to the field." And while they
> were in the field, Cain attacked his brother Abel and
> killed him. (Genesis 4:6–8)

Into what begins as a merely an "unlucky" bad aim, Larkin reads inherent human "failure," the "original sins," first of temptation and then, in the next generation, of violence. The Genesis timeline is as compressed as the poem. Adam "bites" the fruit, the couple are exiled from Eden and, within eight verses, the first murder occurs. Larkin counts on his audience's familiarity with the doctrine of Original Sin and applies it to the most trivial incident of "a miss." Into that miss he reads the entire and inevitable failures of the human race.

Life's inevitable disappointments concern Larkin. Missing the basket is but one, but it is definitive. Biblical allusions assist in the delivery of his insights, but he does not look to religion or its emissaries for reassurance. Still, Larkin is a thoughtful human being and poet; in all human

honesty, he is unable to deny that craving for reassurance.
An explicitly religious poem, "Church-Going" (97–98; see
Appendix), considers the state and future of religious belief and admits that, though his speaker is "bored, uninformed," it nevertheless "Pleases me to stand in silence
here." "Here" is a church at which his speaker has stopped
during a biking holiday. The encounter demonstrates to
the initially cynical visitor that such a traditional edifice
will always draw us. His first response is vague indifference:
"Another church." He mockingly goes to the lectern and
pretends to read the week's lesson, "pronouncing 'Here
endeth' much more loudly than I meant." The modern
agnostic longs to make fun of the church experience, but
something deeper inside—perhaps his conscience, perhaps trained obedience or merely tribal loyalty—corrects
him. He finally has to acquiesce in the spirit that brought
him into the place and made him take off his bicycle clips
"in awkward reverence." No, the honest man within has
to confess: "Someone will forever be surprising/A hunger
in himself to be more serious." People will always "[gravi-
tate] to this ground/Which, he once heard, was proper to
grow wise in." It's a sensitive insight; it reflects his awareness of a role religion can play, balanced against his own
agnosticism. He has no doctrinal axe to grind. Doctrine
and dogma are matters he never addresses, only our felt
needs for "wisdom."

He looks down the years and tries to imagine the
last person who will enter this once-sacred precinct. He
first has fun imagining "some ruin-bibber, randy for antique"—that class of people who get turned on by the obsolete—but then grows more serious. "Or will he be my
representative" who will approach the spot with intellectual respect,

> ...because it held unspilt
> So long and equally what since is found

> Only in separation—marriage, and birth
> And death, and thoughts of these? (48–51)

A church is almost an institutional confirmation that human needs must be addressed. Church at least tried to bring those longings together, a place "in whose blent air all our compulsions meet,/Are recognized, and robed as destinies." A church acknowledges our drives as legitimate and grants them very nearly a sacred legitimacy —"destinies." He then, however, characteristically moves to an ironic final observation. The visible sign that confirms those needs is the "so many dead [that] lie round." The full graveyard around the deteriorating church is a reminder of the longing that churches have tried forever but in the end unsuccessfully to assuage. All he will grant is that the longing is instinctive and permanent.

The poem "Faith Healing" (126; see Appendix) is perhaps Larkin's most sympathetic effort to examine that same craving, matched with a particularly devastating assessment of any chance for its satisfaction. His portrait of the Healer is one whom Americans will recognize from many channels on any given Sunday morning. The man's behavior helps show why religious faith is at once a needed but a useless antidote. One early sign of the man's inadequacy is the way Larkin pictures him, in parts: "rimless glasses, silver hair, dark suit, white collar." We never see the complete man, only his "voice and hands." This is not the fancy poetic technique of synecdoche, in which a part is employed to stand for the whole. Not here. The Faith Healer only comes in parts; his success, like his message is merely partial, never fully achieved. Those hands and that voice do indeed promise those needy souls who come forward a "warm spring rain of loving care." But, alas, the American showman's caring is primarily ostentatious: "Scarcely pausing, [he] goes into a prayer/Directing God about this eye, that knee." That verb "direct" suggests arrogance; what's worse, it tends only to externals, not inner need.

The poet's real concern is with that "loving care's" inadequacy. Its superficiality is poignantly clear when we look at the deep despair of the women who, it seems, try but fail to answer his initial, loving question to each, "Now, dear child, what's wrong?" He moves them through his salvific assembly line at "twenty seconds" each, far too quickly to be able to discern their plights fully. But we readers do have the leisure, through Larkin's more caring vision, to observe their stories. We witness the fragile souls the healer abandons too quickly. "Some stay stiff...with deep hoarse tears...thinking a voice/At last calls them alone." That final word is powerful. It suggests two meanings. One is that they are always craving someone who will single them out (alone; just them) for special attention. The other sense is more distressing: they *are* alone; that aborted calling simply confirms their isolation. One could make a good case that these faceless suffering women are much like the "broken nobodies" whose plights were Jesus' particular care. Larkin's "victims" are merely the usual, contemporary folks for whom life has brought nothing, not even a hint of being loved or cared for. They are not the victims of an imperial system, but their lives are as empty and fruitless.

Larkin answers the healer's ostentatious concern with the rhetorical and sarcastic reply it truly deserves: "What's wrong!...By now, all's wrong." A blessing comes nowhere near addressing, much less satisfying, their needs. Larkin announces the facts of the case: "In everyone there sleeps/A sense of life lived according to love." It sounds as if he intends to analyze that sleeping sense and grant it legitimacy. He admits that "To some it means the difference they could make/By loving others." He is thoughtful enough to recognize that, yes, there are the few who try to give their life meaning by reaching out to others. But, for most of us, "it sweeps [across] /As all they might have done had they been loved." And to that recognized need comes Larkin's uncompromising reply: "That nothing cures."

Larkin is an un-churched modern man for whom religious talk and ritual is, while endlessly tempting, pointless and deceiving. Through him we glimpse life as it is lived—and as it is found painfully inadequate—by modern, post-Christian man and woman. Indeed, Larkin would be worth reading as a rather sad final chapter were it not for his Christian near-contemporary, C. S. Lewis. Larkin provides a portrait of a world where God's kingdom—whether spelled out in the early church's four gospels or glimpsed, as by Shaw, in Christ's actual teachings and work—is of no help.

Jesus would have been horrified at the poet's lack of faith, but might yet have felt a brotherly pang. When I read between the lines of the various gospels, I sense a deeply devout, even intensely zealous Jew who was indeed outraged at the institutional state of his faith under Roman imperial rule. He was an angry man, angry at how much his religious leaders had rendered unto Caesar, as Mark's account of his cleansing of the Temple vividly shows. He could probably relate to Larkin's disgust at what Christian practitioners like the faith healer have become. He would certainly have shared Larkin's pity for those broken and abandoned souls in whom "sleeps a sense of life according to love."

Christ inveighed against Judaism's institutional failures. Larkin laments, though more in sorrow than anger, a Christianity whose vitality is no longer available.

Works Cited

Eliot, T. S. "The Journey of the Magi." P. 1797 in *Norton Anthology of English Literature.* Vol 2. New York: Norton, 1968.

Fitzgerald, F. Scott. *This Side of Paradise.* Bartleby.com: Great
    Books Online. http://www.bartleby.com/115/index.
    html.
Larkin, Philip. *Collected Poems.* Edited with an introduction
    by Anthony Thwaite. Farrar, Straus, Giroux, 1989 (6th
    printing 2000).
Yeats, William Butler. "The Second Coming." P. 1582 in
    Norton Anthology of English Literature. Vol 2. New York:
    Norton, 1968.

9

C. S. Lewis

Modern Orthodoxy

I t should come as no surprise that a modern Christian theologian, university professor and literary critic like Professor C. S. Lewis would be a natural choice to whom to turn for sophisticated literature that nonetheless projects a deeply Christian message. This applies not only to his avowedly spiritual efforts like *Mere Christianity* or *The Problem of Pain*. It also applies to his science fiction works and especially, or perhaps surprisingly, to his works of fantasy for children—*The Chronicles of Narnia*.

One work in that series I find especially profound, theologically speaking, as well as remarkably sophisticated as literature. *The Voyage of the Dawn Treader* in fact offers abundant meat for both literary and theological palates. As it turns out, children's fantasy proves to be an ideal genre for dealing with such thorny issues as personal redemption and spiritual transcendence. Fantasy, which rejects the rules of realism, is a credible way for a writer to entertain the impossible; it need not hew to everyday expectations and physical laws. It is true that the Scottish philosopher David Hume taught us to doubt the impossible, to question purported miracles. But his strictures obviously do not apply to literature. They are foreign above all to fantasy creations aimed at children's fertile imaginations. Fantasy also puts poetic technique like metaphor and simile to good use. It may thus remind us of gospel episodes where the impossible also occurs, fictional narratives inserted to help dramatize a spiritual truth. Jesus, revealing himself as the Christ, calms a storm; he can even walk on water. For Biblical literalists, performing the impossible confirms his divinity; for more reasonable believers, it makes a powerful metaphorical statement about the transformative power of faith.

In short, works written ostensibly for children get permission to explore such impossibilities, and it seems they do so invariably with their artists' creative imagination at full throttle. Youngsters have not yet mastered the rules and restrictions of adult life, much less the sensible conventions of adult literature. Their imaginations are ripe for and fully open to the wonderful—like a land that can be reached by falling into a picture or by stepping into a clothes closet; or a country where time ticks on its own schedule, so visitors from our world cannot know whether ten minutes or five centuries have passed each time they return. Narnia is also a land in which sea serpents crawl the ocean and dragons fly and spout fire. Even better, it is a world in which a particularly unlikeable human child can be transformed into one such dragon and then proceed to achieve moral reformation as a direct result of the shocking metamorphosis. Marvelous opportunities! And Lewis takes full advantage.

Another way of capturing the impossible is (as we have seen) through paradox, a union of opposites that upon inspection proves accurate. Winston Churchill, for instance, observed that "Democracy is the worst form of government yet invented—except for all the other forms that have been tried from time to time." The statement is, when first confronted, an impossibility. It cannot be both. But once we recognize the first half of the statement as an expression of emotional frustration, a deeply-felt helplessness at the difficulties democracy always generates, we can then reconcile it with the fairer appraisal that the prepositional phrase proposes. Both can be accurate. We saw this in Donne's Renaissance poem (one grows pure by being raped) and Chaucer's medieval tale (the old hag becomes beautiful when her wisdom is granted legitimacy). Both artists recognize that an imaginative or fictional paradox is one way for a writer to demonstrated how religion, or the religious sensibility, can operate on the human consciousness and its hard-to-define, much less fathom, psychological operations.

The *Voyage of the Dawn Treader*, like the older, more traditionally Christian works we have examined, explores those mysterious ways in which God moves in approaching, beckoning and transforming the individual soul. Donne knew that God would "knock, breathe, shine and seek to mend." Chaucer's hag reminds Arthur's errant knight of how far he has fallen short of the proper Christian obligations of a man, not to mention a member of the noble Round Table. She reveals herself to him as a creature who both embodies and voices Christ's words and life; it is her firm homily that opens his eyes. Herbert's collared man need only hear the one word "Child" to achieve instantaneous reformation. Scrooge endures a night of prolonged self-inspection brought on by the reminders and lectures of the three visiting spirits. Only Herbert's form of reformation speaks to today's realists; the others posit what are literally impossible creatures—a witch, three ghosts. Yet each of the narratives effects a genuine redemption.

The character at whom the process is aimed in Lewis' tale is Eustace Scrubb, the selfish, narcissistic, spoiled and very modern lad whom we meet in the opening paragraph of the opening chapter. Eustace is the first and most extreme candidate for moral testing in a book that is in fact structured as a series of such moral tests: every character, from the lowly mariners to King Caspian himself, is in turn challenged and found wanting. Particularly eloquent testimony to human inadequacy occurs late in the story when the entire crew sails toward a "Dark Island," a place where dreams come true—not day dreams, however, but nightmares. What they encounter there are their deepest dread and most fallible selves. When it occurs, the crew, to a man, turns tail and flees (197).

Eustace's cousin Lucy, who is making her third Narnian tour, receives her moral reproof directly at the hands of Aslan. Aslan is the wonderful golden Lion who rules this fictional land, a firm but loving creature. In the first story of what became the full set of Chronicles, *The Lion, the Witch and the Wardrobe*, Lewis clearly intends Aslan as a Christ figure. In the subsequent tales, Aslan usually functions as God Himself, though with a human or at least leonine face. Lucy is already a proper and humble young lady, so her reform is effected far more kindly and gently than that of Eustace.

Eustace's transformation from self-involvement to a humble member of a questing community is effectively and movingly rendered. Lewis takes a further, almost satirical step in making young Scrubb emblematic, through his parents, of the ills of our sterile, unimaginative, "modern" world, circa 1950. He thereby mitigates some of the lad's guilt by showing his parents' responsibility for it. Eustace absorbs what Lewis sees as their wholly self-oriented selves. They have raised their only child to learn about "exports and imports and governments and drains" (92). The Scrubbs are also committed teetotalers, non-smokers, and vegetarians, their diets almost as unappealing as those of Golding's Neanderthals. Windows in their home are always open and the rooms are sparsely furnished: such is the sterile, frigid, too healthful environment in which Eustace has grown up. "Very up-to-date and advanced people," is Lewis' succinct and dismissive summary (1). Time of course takes its toll on an earlier era's satiric judgments: what seemed effete and unnatural to Lewis, the traditional

and rather Victorian Oxford don, today are draw increasingly popular approval. Today's behavioral Puritans are
having the last laugh.

Perhaps most telling, the parents do not require their
son to call them "Father" and "Mother"; they insist instead
on Harold and Alberta. They have, in short, given up traditional family hierarchy and substituted an unearned
democratic equality. They have even banished magic from
their household; indeed, their greatest sin lies in stultifying the powers of the imagination. They saw to it he "had
read only the wrong books" (89). The ones he read "were
weak on dragons," nothing with any adventure or appeals
to the imagination. Aptly, the magical picture into which
the children fall at the start of the novel, though given to
the parents as a wedding gift, has been relegated to the
back of the house (4). Lewis seems to equate this reliance
on the modern with the squelching of the imagination,
which Lewis sees as the hallmark and curse of modern
blandness. But such squelching cannot succeed forever.
No matter how far out of sight we may suppress our longing for the transcendent, the chance for it to re-emerge is
never wholly erased. Fortunately for Eustace, his cousins,
the two Narnian veterans Lucy and Edmund, pay him a
visit. They thus serve as exemplars of daring, of the love
of adventure, and of the deep religious sense of humility that has sprung from their encounters with Aslan. The
picture is the only one in the house they admire. It proves
to be the one chink in the Scrubb family's sterile modern
life, their house's sole pathway to the redemption Narnia
offers.

Unwillingly transported into the magical realm,
Eustace also brings with him a sizable share of British imperial arrogance. He demands to be "put ashore" to report
what he considers a kidnapping to the "nearest British con-
sul" (28). He cannot stand the lively and bouncing "Dawn

Treader." It fails to measure up to his notion of a true vessel: a huge sea-going craft which for him means you do not even know you are at sea (31). There we behold another instance of our age's avoidance of true adventure: going to sea is like staying in a floating hotel. Eustace, trained by Harold and Alberta, represents conventional notions of advanced civilization and a divorce from older, more natural values and habits.

A most convenient way for revealing the inner Eustace, his real personality and values, is his diary; it's an effective literary strategy, as it provides handy insight into Eustace's mind, which he reveals with unfortunate accuracy. Through its pages, we see his moral and behavioral estrangement from the rest of the company on the quest. I do not think Lewis is condemning the habit of keeping a journal, though he might well see it as typical of our era's narcissism, our obsession with constant self-inspection.

The premise of the quest undertaken by the characters is this: Caspian, newly crowned King of Narnia, sees it as his mission to sail east in search of seven lords whom his evil Uncle Miraz had banished. They were his father's dear friends, so the quest is thus an effort to reintegrate both a family's and a nation's past, as well as to prove the son his father's worthy heir. It is, shall we say, a far nobler endeavor than the punitive one imposed on Chaucer's erring knight. Both, however, prove deeply educational, morally speaking.

When Eustace starts writing, an intense storm has just decimated the "Dawn Treader's" supplies. Water rations have been imposed. Eustace, however, finds himself thirsty one night and wants to help himself to that restricted water. He tries first to excuse his behavior through selfish rationalization. His words, "I never dreamed this rationing would apply to a sick man" (76) show his rejection of moral responsibility. He even pretends that this selfish act sprang from charity: "I would have woken the others only I thought it would be selfish to wake them." He kids himself further that the reason he "took great care not to disturb Caspian and Edmund" was that "they'd been sleeping badly....I always try to consider others whether they are nice to me or not" (77). He knows the vocabulary of concern, but employs it in the service of self-deception and self-indulgence.

His rationalizations support selfish need, and he clothes them with the pretence of consideration and fellow-feeling. Now *that,* Lewis would insist, is the one quality Eustace is most sorely lacking. His estrangement from the voyagers' fellowship will be precisely the mental habit that needs curing. It's the same psychological process we saw in the speaker of Donne's Holy Sonnet, though he at least is able to recognize "the devices and desires of [his] heart" objectively and honestly. "Reason" is God's "viceroy;" He gives it us as a guard against evil, but inevitably "it is captiv'd, and proves weak or untrue." When the sin of self-indulgence takes us over, we corrupt our God-given reason and put it to ever more selfish, ever more sinful rationalizations.

Eustace's true challenge—and his adventures—begin on the lonely island where the "Treader" docks for repairs. It is meet and right that he undergo his test alone, having snuck away from the hard work demanded of the crew. He has, characteristically, refused his share in the community much in the way his parents have divorced their ethical priorities from traditional societal standards. Lewis does note, though, that, as Eustace is scrabbling hard to get away from his fellows, the remarkable energy and determination he exhibits are already a sign of the positive effects of his "new life" (82). As in the case of Chaucer's hag, who promised to change herself in "three days," the religious connotations of "new life" hint at Lewis' more theological purposes. Narnia is already restoring Eustace, at least in body.

In his instinctive avoidance of communal obligations, however, Eustace's thoughts are concentrated solely on Eustace. When he finds himself lost in the rocky, barren crags above the harbor, he suddenly grows desperate to get back, for he assumes the crew will leave without him. Lewis, the literary artist, makes good use of the landscape here. Its barrenness—the "burnt patches" and "grim peaks" (88)—duplicates in physical terms the quality of life the boy has lived with his parents. More vitally, his fear of being abandoned reveals how profoundly he lacks a comprehension of fellowship. Even the member of the crew who most disapproves of him, Reepicheep the Mouse, upbraids a colleague who mutters "good riddance" at the boy's disappearance. No, he says, "Master Rhince, you never spoke a word that becomes you less. The creature…is of the Queen's blood and while he is one of our fellowship, it concerns our honour to find him" (94). That notion of fellowship is vital. Fellowship is, after all, Christian principles in action—selfless dedication to a community. That is the same communal ideal Faulkner paints and praises in rural Mississippi; it echoes directly the values spoken by the loyal thane Macbeth and dramatized in the working out of his tragedy. Tempted by his wife to thirst for the crown and thereby be more "the man," Macbeth makes the firm denial. "I dare do all that may become a man. Who dares do more is none" (I.vii.46–47).

The key concept, there for Macbeth and here voiced by Reepicheep, is that of "becoming." There are, in truth, fixed and abiding standards of behavior. Humanity is expected to adhere to them; once you go beyond them you have betrayed the principles that organize a healthy society. Your values do not "become" you; once you give them up, you grow into a monster and dispose of your humanity as Macbeth's wife sarcastically reminds him: "What beast was it then/That made you break this enterprise to me?/When you durst [dared] do it, then you were a man" (47–49). 'Daring' like that does not fit the standards of the community of which he is a part. Later, Macbeth's inability to say "amen," as we saw when he is heading towards King Duncan's chamber, confirms that devastating divorce. Reepicheep voices that same firm definitive criterion. Once one is part of the fellowship, one accepts all members as valuable members; no "riddance" of him or her can be "good," whatever one may think of that person's particulars. The community certifies all its members as legitimate participants. Lewis cleverly uses the one non-human of the story, the valiant and, by theological standards, infallible Mouse, to voice these ideals. Being of a different species, he avoids human fallibility. It is likewise appropriate at the end of the tale that "Reep" becomes the only Narnian creature ever to go directly to heaven—Aslan's country. He enjoys an ascension without the inconvenience of death.

Lewis now repeatedly alternates scenes between the lost Eustace and the worried crew, but the heart of the episode, this author's central theological and literary mission, is to dramatize Eustace's redemption. The boy ends up in a dragon's lair and is, not surprisingly, pleased to discover the treasure the beast has accumulated. A dragon's symbolic role, it would seem, is to embody utter acquisitiveness. That's the beast's significance in the early Anglo-Saxon epic *Beowulf* and Lewis' friend J. R. R. Tolkien puts it to the same use in *The Hobbit*. Eustace reveals at least one benefit of his practical, economic training as his first thoughts on seeing the gold are fiscal. "They don't have tax here.... And you don't have to give treasure to the government." In the remainder of this soliloquy, Eustace uses those most selfish pronouns, "I" and "myself," seven times (93), confirming yet again the extent to which his ego governs his thinking.

Lewis takes his leisurely time showing Eustace sleeping on the hoard, finding the place more and more congenial, but eventually waking to the horrifying realization: he has *become* a dragon. That, clearly, is the wrong kind of becoming! Of all the improbable things that occur in this make-believe world, this takes the cake. It is remarkable, nay impossible. But that impossible change is the perfect dramatic vehicle for the author's psychological, moral and ultimately theological purposes. Even then, Eustace feels—characteristically again—a brief spurt of relief, a sense of power, and a longing for revenge. "He could get even with Edmund and Caspian now."

But it is at that very moment of achieved ego that he comes to his moral senses. "He wanted to be friends. He wanted to get back among humans and talk and laugh and share things." He is at last craving that crucial fellowship that Lewis considers to lie at the heart of the Christian ethos. His new "appalling loneliness" produces for the first time both an honest self-appraisal and a wholly novel appreciation of the others. He realized they "had not been fiends at all" and, better yet, "began to wonder if he had been such a nice person as he always assumed" (98). We are starting to see the beneficial effects of an agonizing transformation that Edmund will later rightly summarize, paradoxically but aptly, as "beastly."

We soon discover how appropriate that dragon conversion is when, without thinking, Eustace devours the dead dragon beside him. Gross? Yes. But Lewis gives it a symbolic explanation. Dragons' favorite food is "fresh dragon" which is why, he points out, "You so seldom find more than one dragon in a country" (100). Dragons are loners; one of their greatest pleasures lies in destroying their own kind. In contrast, Macbeth's witches have evil purposes, true, but toward each other they are sisterly. When one lends another a wind to help her harass a sailor, the other thanks her: "th'art kind." That adjective means, as we know, "one of us." Dragons, though, are by nature at odds with that very concept. Eustace's behavior as a boy has been of a similarly selfish kind, visiting at least psychological cruelty on anyone in his vicinity.

It is perhaps poetic justice that a second-generation vegetarian becomes not only a full-fledged carnivore but a cannibal to boot; it may be further an apt punishment for us modern "scrubbed" humans, as we seek to erase from our consciousness any sense of our inherent carnality. It is further appropriate that Eustace discover his new self by staring into a pool. It is quite literally, if horrifically, a place for reflection. Not only do we see the parallel with Narcissus, but we suspect and hope that Eustace will use the period of reflection for coming to a new, redeemed sense of himself.

Once Eustace has begun the critical self-appraisal that his transformation uniquely provides, he returns, though still in dragon form, to his shipmates in abject humility. He initiates the long, slow process of reintegration. Once they discover who he is, they try to welcome him back. As one might expect in this magic land, they seem to take it in stride that a boy can become a dragon. It's the way their world works. The situation also allows Lewis to practice his effective literary craft, the gift for making such fictional impossibilities credible. For example, when the dragon boy expresses his anguish at his predicament, "he thumped his tail in the sea and everyone skipped back (some of the sailors with ejaculations I will not put down in writing)" (106). Lewis makes it seem perfectly logical, first, that an unhappy dragon would thump its tail with wild abandon. It seems just as believable, second, that hardened, salty sailors would express their anger appropriately. Their unprintable comments add to the believability of Eustace's wildly unlikely (to us realistic folks) predicament.

His punishment lasts far longer than those of Chaucer's knight, Herbert's priest or Scrooge, but he does learn to be helpful. He finds tall trees for the ship's new mast; his fiery insides provide warmth and comfort for the company at night. He flies across the island on useful scouting expeditions and kills animals they will need for the resumed voyage, but does so most humanely. His new experience of being liked, says Lewis, is about the only redeeming feature of his new life and self. First, he must live out his spiritual despair: Eustace "was almost afraid to be alone with himself and yet he was ashamed to be with others" (109).

So he still needs to be cured. For *all* their sakes. For one thing, the crew knows he is far too big to fit on their diminutive vessel. The realization drives home to him yet again what a nuisance he is; it makes him realize still more forcefully now much of one he always *has* been. Just as the gold bracelet he slipped on as a greedy boy in the dragon's lair now eats into his skin as a dragon, this self-loathing "ate into his mind" (110). To the joint fellowship's rescue comes Aslan, in what is doctrinally Lewis' most profound move. Eustace shows up to Edmund late one night, back in his normal form, but the story he tells is both harrowing and reassuring. He tells Edmund of a dream he's had (shades of Scrooge again) in which a lion (*we* know who it is) appears to him and speaks, though he never actually talks. It's another magical and redemptive paradox, one that may remind us of Jeremiah's encounter with that "still, small voice." The lion carries Eustace to a paradisiacal garden—"trees and fruit and everything" (114). This is pretty clearly a return to Eden, at least in spirit, and the word "everything" means far more than the vague word we customarily use when we just mean "et cetera." No, here we see that Aslan, the stern but loving God, is indeed a catholic provider.

Somehow, Eustace knows he can and should undertake the needed transformation Aslan recommends and so he proceeds to try to strip himself of his scaly skin. He even digs a bit deeper, knowing how much of his old bad self he needs to shed. He is proud of himself: "my whole skin started peeking off beautifully, like it does after an illness" (114). The simile is perfect; Eustace is returning to moral health by ridding himself of his sick old self. But now comes the catch. He looks down at the shed layer and realizes he is still encased in thick dragon hide. He tries again, strips again; it slowly dawns on him that it is not going to be enough. I believe Lewis' point here is psychological as well as doctrinal. We cannot cure ourselves; self-analysis and confession are good for the soul but are not and cannot be finally redemptive; self-help groups or psychiatrists, with whom we modern, fallen folk share our ills and try to resolve them through talk, may feel good, but they do not cure. The therapist must yield to the redeemer.

For that we need God. It is Aslan who has to redeem Eustace. "The very first tear that he made was so deep that I thought it had gone right into my heart" (115). Well, in a symbolic sense it has. It is thorough-going and intense, as was needed for Donne's sinful speaker, who needed to be ravished to be pure. The result for Eustace is like Scrooge's; he is filled with delight. Scrooge felt like a baby. He finds the kid in the street "delightful." Eustace sees and feels his real arms again. "I know they've no muscle and are pretty mouldy compared with Caspian's, but I was so glad to see them" (116). Delight in his old self is combined with a humble recognition of his own inadequacy.

Work Cited

Lewis, C. S. *The Voyage of the Dawn Treader.* New York: Harper Trophy, 2002.

Appendix of Religious Poems

George Herbert

The Collar

I struck the board, and cried, "No more;
                    I will abroad!
    What? shall I ever sigh and pine?
My lines and life are free, free as the rode,
    Loose as the wind, as large as store.
                Shall I be still in suit?
    Have I no harvest but a thorn
    To let me blood, and not restore
What I have lost with cordial fruit?
                        Sure there was wine
        Before my sighs did dry it; there was corn
        Before my tears did drown it.
    Is the year only lost to me?
        Have I no bays to crown it?
No flowers, no garlands gay? All blasted?
                All wasted?
    Not so, my heart; but there is fruit,
                And thou hast hands.
        Recover all thy sigh-blown age
On double pleasures: leave thy cold dispute
Of what is fit, and not. Forsake thy cage,
                Thy rope of sands,
Which petty thoughts have made, and made to thee
    Good cable, to enforce and draw,
                And be thy law,
    While thou didst wink and wouldst not see.
                Away! take heed;
                I will abroad.

Call in thy death's-head there; tie up thy fears.
He that forbears
To suit and serve his need,
Deserves his load."
But as I raved and grew more fierce and wild
At every word,
Methought I heard one calling, *Child!*
And I replied, *My Lord.*

John Donne

Batter my Heart, Three-Personed God

Batter my heart, three-personed God; for You
As yet but knock, breathe, shine, and seek to mend;
That I may rise and stand, o'erthrow me, and bend
Your force, to break, blow, burn, and make me new.
I, like an usurped town, to another due,
Labor to admit You, but Oh, to no end!
Reason, Your viceroy in me, me should defend,
But is captived, and proves weak or untrue.
Yet dearly I love You, and would be loved fain,
But am betrothed unto Your enemy ;
Divorce me, untie or break that knot again,
Take me to You, imprison me, for I,
Except You enthrall me, never shall be free,
Nor ever chaste, except You ravish me.

Andrew Marvell

A Dialogue Between Soul and Body

SOUL: O, who shall from this dungeon raise
A soul enslaved so many ways?
With bolts of bones, that fettered stands
In feet, and manacled in hands;
Here blinded with an eye, and there
Deaf with the drumming of an ear;
A soul hung up, as 'twere, in chains
Of nerves, and arteries, and veins;
Tortured, besides each other part,
In a vain head, and double heart?

BODY: O, who shall me deliver whole,
From bonds of this tyrannic soul?
Which, stretched upright, impales me so
That mine own precipice I go;
And warms and moves this needless frame,
(A fever could but do the same),
And, wanting where its spite to try,
Has made me live to let me die
A body that could never rest,
Since this ill spirit it possessed.

SOUL: What magic could me thus confine
Within another's grief to pine?
Where, whatsoever it complain,
I feel, that cannot feel, the pain;
And all my care itself employs,
That to preserve which me destroys;
Constrained not only to endure

Diseases, but, what's worse, the cure;
And, ready oft the port to gain,
Am shipwrecked into health again.

BODY: But Physic yet could never reach
The maladies thou me dost teach;
Whom first the cramp of hope does tear,
And then the palsy shakes of fear;
The pestilence of love does heat,
Or hatred's hidden ulcer eat;
Joy's cheerful madness does perplex,
Or sorrow's other madness vex;
Which knowledge forces me to know,
And memory will not forego;
What but a soul could have the wit
To build me up for sin so fit?
So architects do square and hew
Green trees that in the forest grew.

John Donne

A Valediction Forbidding Mourning

As virtuous men pass mildly away,
    And whisper to their souls to go,
Whilst some of their sad friends do say,
    "The breath goes now," and some say, "No."

So let us melt, and make no noise,   5
    No tear-floods, nor sigh-tempests move;
'Twere profanation of our joys
    To tell the laity our love.

Moving of the earth brings harms and fears;
    Men reckon what it did, and meant;   10
But trepidation of the spheres,
    Though greater far, is innocent.

Dull sublunary lovers' love
    (Whose soul is sense) cannot admit
Absence, because it doth remove   15
    Those things which elemented it.

But we by a love so much refined
    That ourselves know not what it is,
Inter-assurèd of the mind,
    Care less, eyes, lips, and hands to miss.   20

Our two souls therefore, which are one,
    Though I must go, endure not yet
A breach, but an expansion,
    Like gold to airy thinness beat.

If they be two, they are two so   25
     As stiff twin compasses are two;
Thy soul, the fixed foot, makes no show
     To move, but doth, if the other do.

And though it in the center sit,
     Yet when the other far doth roam,   30
It leans, and hearkens after it,
     And grows erect, as that comes home.

Such wilt thou be to me, who must,
     Like the other foot, obliquely run;
Thy firmness makes my circle just,   35
     And makes me end where I begun.

Philip Larkin

Faith Healing

Slowly the women file to where he stands
Upright in rimless glasses, silver hair,
Dark suit, white collar. Stewards tirelessly
Persuade them onwards to his voice and hands,
Within whose warm spring rain of loving care
Each dwells some twenty seconds. *Now, dear child,
What's wrong,* the deep American voice demands,
And, scarcely pausing, goes into a prayer
Directing God about this eye, that knee.
Their heads are clasped abruptly; then, exiled

Like losing thoughts, they go in silence; some
Sheepishly stray, not back into their lives
Just yet; but some stay stiff, twitching and loud
With deep hoarse tears, as if a kind of dumb
And idiot child within them still survives
To re-awake at kindness, thinking a voice
At last calls them alone, that hands have come
To lift and lighten; and such joy arrives
Their thick tongues blort, their eyes squeeze grief, a crowd
Of huge unheard answers jam and rejoice—

What's wrong! Moustached in flowered frocks they shake:
By now, all's wrong. In everyone there sleeps
A sense of life lived according to love.
To some it means the difference they could make
By loving others, but across most it sweeps
As all they might have done had they been loved.

That nothing cures. An immense slackening ache,
As when, thawing, the rigid landscape weeps,
Spreads slowly through them—that, and the voice above
Saying *Dear child,* and all time has disproved.

Philip Larkin

Ambulances

Closed like confessionals, they thread
Loud noons of cities, giving back
None of the glances they absorb.
Light glossy grey, arms on a plaque,
They come to rest at any kerb:
All streets in time are visited.

Then children strewn on steps or road,
Or women coming from the shops
Past smells of different dinners, see
A wild white face that overtops
Red stretcher-blankets momently
As it is carried in and stowed,

And sense the solving emptiness
That lies just under all we do,
And for a second get it whole,
So permanent and blank and true.
The fastened doors recede. Poor soul,
They whisper at their own distress;

For borne away in deadened air
May go the sudden shut of loss
Round something nearly at an end,
And what cohered in it across
The years, the unique random blend
Of families and fashions, there

At last begin to loosen. Far
From the exchange of love to lie
Unreachable inside a room
The traffic parts to let go by
Brings closer what is left to come,
And dulls to distance all we are.

Philip Larkin

Church Going

Once I am sure there's nothing going on
I step inside, letting the door thud shut.
Another church: matting, seats, and stone,
And little books; sprawlings of flowers, cut
For Sunday, brownish now; some brass and stuff
Up at the holy end; the small neat organ;
And a tense, musty, unignorable silence,
Brewed God knows how long. Hatless, I take off
My cycle-clips in awkward reverence,

Move forward, run my hand around the font.
From where I stand, the roof looks almost new—
Cleaned or restored? Someone would know: I don't.
Mounting the lectern, I peruse a few
Hectoring large-scale verses, and pronounce
'Here endeth' much more loudly than I'd meant.
The echoes snigger briefly. Back at the door
I sign the book, donate an Irish sixpence,
Reflect the place was not worth stopping for.

Yet stop I did: in fact I often do,
And always end much at a loss like this,
Wondering what to look for; wondering, too,
When churches fall completely out of use
What we shall turn them into, if we shall keep
A few cathedrals chronically on show,
Their parchment, plate, and pyx in locked cases,
And let the rest rent-free to rain and sheep.
Shall we avoid them as unlucky places?

Or, after dark, will dubious women come
To make their children touch a particular stone;
Pick simples for a cancer; or on some
Advised night see walking a dead one?
Power of some sort or other will go on
In games, in riddles, seemingly at random;
But superstition, like belief, must die,
And what remains when disbelief has gone?
Grass, weedy pavement, brambles, buttress, sky,

A shape less recognizable each week,
A purpose more obscure. I wonder who
Will be the last, the very last, to seek
This place for what it was; one of the crew
That tap and jot and know what rood-lofts were?
Some ruin-bibber, randy for antique,
Or Christmas-addict, counting on a whiff
Of gown-and-bands and organ-pipes and myrrh?
Or will he be my representative,

Bored, uninformed, knowing the ghostly silt
Dispersed, yet tending to this cross of ground
Through suburb scrub because it held unspilt
So long and equably what since is found
Only in separation—marriage, and birth,
And death, and thoughts of these—for whom was built
This special shell? For, though I've no idea
What this accoutred frowsty barn is worth,
It pleases me to stand in silence here;

A serious house on serious earth it is,
In whose blent air all our compulsions meet,
Are recognised, and robed as destinies.
And that much never can be obsolete,
Since someone will forever be surprising

A hunger in himself to be more serious,
And gravitating with it to this ground,
Which, he once heard, was proper to grow wise in,
If only that so many dead lie round.

Index to Scriptural References

Author and Subject Index

About the Author

Jamie Spencer (Ph.D., Washington University) is Professor of English at St. Louis Community College. He has taught various adult education classes on Philip Larkin and C. S. Lewis, and reviews books and music for the *St. Louis Post Dispatch* and *The Riverfront Times.*

CPSIA information can be obtained at www.ICGtesting.com
Printed in the USA
267344BV00004B/3/P